ART, CULTURE, & EDUCATION

COUNTERPOINTS

Studies in the Postmodern Theory of Education

Joe L. Kincheloe and Shirley R. Steinberg
General Editors

Vol. 212

PETER LANG
New York • Washington, D.C./Baltimore • Bern
Frankfurt am Main • Berlin • Brussels • Vienna • Oxford

Karel Rose &
Joe L. Kincheloe

Art, Culture, & Education

Artful Teaching in a Fractured Landscape

PETER LANG
New York • Washington, D.C./Baltimore • Bern
Frankfurt am Main • Berlin • Brussels • Vienna • Oxford

Library of Congress Cataloging-in-Publication Data

Rose, Karel.
Art, culture, and education: artful teaching
in a fractured landscape / Karel Rose, Joe L. Kincheloe.
p. cm. — (Counterpoints; v. 212)
Includes bibliographical references and index.
1. Art and society—United States—History—20th century. 2. Art—
Study and teaching—United States. 3. Educational sociology—United States.
4. Crimes without victims—United States. I. Kincheloe, Joe L. II. Title.
III. Counterpoints (New York, N.Y.); v. 212.
N72.S6R68 700'.1'03—dc21 2002156548
ISBN 978-0-8204-5745-1
ISSN 1058-1634

Bibliographic information published by **Die Deutsche Bibliothek**.
Die Deutsche Bibliothek lists this publication in the "Deutsche
Nationalbibliografie"; detailed bibliographic data is available
on the Internet at http://dnb.ddb.de/.

Cover design by Joni Holst

Once more for Shirley and Murray

And for our students

Table of Contents

Preface

Karel Rose

This is a book about culture, education and the arts. In August 2001, we thought that we had reached some temporary closure on these topics and their interrelationships. Then September 11, 2001, happened! What now to say about culture, education and the arts? What do we tell the children? What has gone wrong in a world that breeds such atrocities with regularity? How can the powers of art help us to understand, cope and heal? Maybe we should just scoop up the remains of the day and listen to Mozart? Or should we attend to our potter's wheel and fashion both a pot and a quiet center within ourselves? We describe in ensuing chapters aesthetic cries of pain in literature, visual arts and in ceremonies that involve dance and music. We write about the importance of sacred spaces and how people gather to share their communal grief at makeshift street memorials as well as at grander structures that honor those who died in the Holocaust and the many conflagrations that have besieged the world. We have tried to show that when Billy Holiday sings, "Strange Fruit," jazz and blues may open an aesthetic window onto our anguished history. Each culture does it differently, but the imaginative power of the arts has often played a role in helping people give a form to their disbelief enabling them to slowly climb out of the depths of grief. After the bombing of the World Trade Center, there was not only a hole in the New York skyline but a hole in our hearts for those who had been consumed by the fires that humanity's shameful history has perpetuated. As the smoke slowly clears, it is apparent that we must come to terms with what it means to live in the world together, whether in the next town or across continents. Now more than ever we need the insights and imagination of artists from all cultures to help us see better in this new political terrain.

For some time, it has been apparent to those of us whose lives are spent on college campuses that many students are disengaged from the world outside their immediate concerns. Their goals are narrowly restricted to climbing into the realm of the affluent or retaining their birthrights. Many studies document that on the more prestigious campuses students are even less connected to the world outside their personal zip codes than their counterparts in public institutions. Maybe September 11 will change all that and students and their professors will recognize that the economic template is not the yardstick by which we can measure success or even power. Violations against race, gender, ethnicity and class begin in the home and the classroom and then play out in the larger society. Educators and artists, though some feel that the latter may be entitled to their indifference, need to labor as tirelessly as the rescue workers at the World Trade Center to contribute to the ideas, dialogue and contemplations that could save our children and ultimately the world. Yes, educators have a mission now more than ever.

In this book, we talk about the power of the arts to simultaneously touch our feelings and intellect. Over two thousand years ago, Aristotle noted that as rational animals we have political agendas. He believed that this power of rationality should guide conduct to create what he called the good community. Time has proved him both right and wrong. Classrooms as well as boardrooms are the places where we model this conduct as we listen to each other, negotiate, share our songs and stories and decide about teaching everyone that the "other" is indeed us. On the cutting edge of this new time, teachers need to demonstrate the courage necessary for creating a new world community. Some of us will do it through words, others with images, while many will sing and dance their joy and pain. We agree with the Polish poet, Czeslaw Milosz when he says, "What is poetry. . .which does not save nations?"

The arts are a double-edged sword; they point and simultaneously are pointed at. Democratic values may emerge from or be obscured by the form and content of a work of art or from its interpreters. The artist may send out multiple voices or be indifferent about the message. Teachers, however, are committed to questioning the script and do not have the luxury of indifference. Teaching has never been a neutral activity. Despite their pale public persona, teachers can be tigers who wield considerable power. Who doesn't remember a teacher who made a difference? What child hasn't said to a parent with new authority, "My teacher told me so."

Teachers change the world one student at a time. At their best, teachers inspire human concern, advocate for universal rights and obligate students to participate in the social fabric of their time. We worry that many teachers feel voiceless and "dumbed down" by their own educations and teach much in the way that they have been taught. Throughout this book, we have noted how art, an intellectually rigorous activity, encourages higher order thinking and scholarship in both teachers and their students.

We anticipate that diverse and richer encounters with art will help educators to think outside the cardboard container and challenge positive notions of an unchanging and essential body of knowledge. In the light of modern history, it is critical that we conceptualize teaching from multiple perspectives and learn from the art of Africa, the Middle East, Native Americans and indigenous artists from around the world. Catching the bus of multiple perspectives prepares us to historicize our insights with understandings about sociocultural divisions and the power relations that inscribe them. Encounters with art provide us with the cognitive benefits of viewing a phenomenon from a number of vantage points that confront difference. We can no longer languish in the comfort of a home furnished with zip-coded ways of thinking which pander to a cognitive agoraphobia. We hope our readers will disrupt their thinking long enough to consider whether their house is a mausoleum of assumptions about teaching, diversity and justice. In every chapter of this book, we ask you to unpack your suitcases. Artists can assist you in this task. There is no such thing as "outsider" art if it opens your eyes. The term itself is a cultural construction.

We raise questions about how the artist challenges ethical values, rather than notions of "good" and "bad," "beautiful" and "ugly." It was the "Sensation" exhibit in 1999, one of the most written about U.S. art events of the twentieth century, and our own teaching responsibilities that provided us with the rationale for this book. "Sensation" changed our thinking and it changed many of our students. As a result, we braid together with even greater fervor the worlds of aesthetics, arts and culture into our teaching. We encourage teachers and students to engage the challenges and terrors that contemporary life brings forth and that art reflects upon. We encourage teachers and students to consider the feelings and moral issues that emerge from world events so that complex ethical questions suffuse classroom conversations. We refrain from making the distinction between what is "good" and what is "right." The bloodiest wars are often fought in the name of what is "right." Our thinking is informed by the writing of William H. Gass, who notes that ethics are always present in behaviors. Hatred, brutality and killing result not because of the absence of ethics (everyone has ethics), but because of the "others'" blindness to the "right" beliefs or the "right" acts.

We describe how we have visited museums with our students so that they may appreciate that school is only one of many educational settings. We want them to recognize that museums are not tombs but living repositories of cultural movements and events with educational intentions. All people, not just those with political or aesthetic authority, need to claim the privilege of making artistic and cognitive judgments. Museums, theaters and even the streets are learning centers. They are places where students can spend the day, even the night. (The Denver Art Museum has sleepovers for elementary schoolchildren.) The Seattle Art Museum invites schoolchildren to curate exhibits. Museums, like schools, can be artful, communal places which cater to a personal and public self-awareness bringing together people and artifacts from different sociocultural contexts. A museum experience can be likened to the difference between watching a video at home or "going to the movies" where others are present and integral to the experience.

As we write, the controversy over what is art and who decides is being waged with new fervor. Art can be dangerous because it makes us think in new ways. Someone is always calling for censorship, for "decency" panels, for the curbing of freedoms. The artist is publicly taken to task, but it is really the message of the artist that frightens the censor. Notwithstanding, artists because of their sensitivity are often impelled to respond to the happy moments and joyful rites of passage as well as the violent and shameful crimes against humanity. At the site, where the World Trade Center stood, dozens of people have managed to set up easels. Others sit writing poetry and many continue to photograph what they find hard to believe. It is the way in which they can best make sense of an atrocious tragedy. People have many dimensions, and a single event may catalyze new understandings. Rudolph Giuliani, the former mayor of New York City, for example, whose policies about artistic freedom and censorship disturbed us, did show a truly heroic persona demonstrating courage and empathy throughout the Twin Towers' catastrophe. We extend to him our greatest respect in this matter.

Art has always had a role interpreting the social and political events of our time. Protest art about the Holocaust, the African Diaspora, apartheid and ethnic cleansing as well as feminist art cries out against silence and scripting providing examples of the ways artists mediate between an abstract world and individual needs. The media are artful and so are the propaganda machines for all regimes which deliver a highly specific agenda. It is our view that teachers, as the storytellers of the culture, are powerful mediators. For this reason, educators need to continue to read the books of the "other" as sacred texts, dialogue with "outsiders," gather in circles to tell stories, paint, sing, dance and perpetuate grand conversations in classrooms and in public spaces so that all voices are included.

one

artful teaching in a "sensational" context

Joe L. Kincheloe

Karel and I were ready in August 1999 to teach our new undergraduate honors class, "High and Low Art: Good and Bad Taste." Our syllabus was troubling us, as we both wanted to see who our students were and how they would react to our initial lessons before locking in the activities and assignments for the semester. Nevertheless, we ordered our books: Toby Clark's *Art and Propaganda in the Twentieth Century*, Paul du Gay's et al.'s *Doing Cultural Studies* and my book with co-editors Shirley Steinberg, Nelson Rodriguez and Ronald Chennault, *White Reign: Deploying Whiteness in America*. Karel hit the pedagogical road running with her questions about the relationships of art, beauty and culture—questions central to her throughout her teaching career. She engaged students in the nature of art and beauty, asking them to bring a beautiful object to class and explain what they thought was beautiful about it.

Her enthusiasm was contagious as our students responded to her thoughtful attentiveness and heightened curiosity. We recognized immediately that our class was filled with highly motivated honors students who were accustomed to academic success and exacting assignments. To challenge some of the students' comfortable assumptions about the purposes of art, the nature of beauty and the relationship between art and beauty, Karel and I began to devise questions and experiences that blurred traditional boundaries, the borders separating high and low art and delineation of good and bad taste. I assigned filmmaker John Waters' spoof of the New York high art scene, *Pecker*, and Karel arranged a class trip to the Museum of Modern Art to view the acclaimed "Fame After Photography" exhibit—two interestingly interactive endeavors.

By the latter half of September students had read the first two chapters of Clark's *Art and Propaganda* and Shirley Steinberg's and my introductory chapter in *White Reign*, "Addressing the Crisis of Whiteness: Reconfiguring White Identity in a Pedagogy of Whiteness." In relation to these readings Karel and I asked students to familiarize themselves with the terms modernism, postmodernism, aesthetics, hermeneutics and epistemology. By the fourth class meeting we were getting ready to take the students down the curvy road to transgressive art and the social, cultural and political dynamics that motivated its production and shaped its reception. Then on September 22 Mayor Rudolph Giuliani—as if he were coordinating his actions with our class assignments—called a press conference to attack the Brooklyn Museum's coming show "Sensation." Our best laid plans for "High and Low Art: Good and Bad Taste" flew out the window with the firestorm that the mayor ignited. We scrambled to take advantage of the unique opportunity presented us.

Of course, this book is a result of our effort to address this opportunity, our attempt to think through the pedagogical dimensions of the questions we wanted to raise in our course. It does not comprehensively discuss the "Sensation" controversy, but it always comes back to the issues the exhibit and the controversy surrounding it raised and continue to raise. Concerns with art, teaching, culture, politics and cognition ran through our class and the "Sensation" controversy and keep operating to shape the cosmos of contemporary art and American society in the first decade of the twenty-first century. Through the lenses of these issues, Karel and I agreed that there was much to learn about the act of teaching—teaching art no doubt but also teaching in general and the social, cultural, cognitive and political dynamics that always frame it. Indeed, in this electric, highly charged context, we thought that it might be easier for observers to discern these complex pedagogical issues than in less emotional and less publicly exposed situations. We decided to take advantage of the opportunities presented: This book is the result.

The Power of Art: "I Have Never Been So Offended"

One of my major goals in this book is to document the power of art, its capacity to inspire, offend, enrage and transform. In our study of the role of art Karel and I maintain that art as expressed in a variety of venues including museums, galleries and art shows but even more significantly in the artistic imagery in movies, TV and popular music plays an unprecedented role in constructing American culture, politics and education. Thus, with these concerns in mind I want to look at the complex interactions connecting art, culture, politics, cognition and education in relation to the social power of art. In the first decade of the twenty-first century educators, politicians and the American public at large are not sufficiently aware of these relationships. Americans will not develop the ability to reflect on who we are as a society, to make compelling projections about the future we want to build, or to conceptualize the type of people we want to become until we develop a more rigorous understanding of the influence of these artistic representations.

Artistic images have an uncanny, almost shamanic power to offend people. In retaliation individuals often attack the image. Numerous people desecrated or attempted to desecrate various pieces in "Sensation," both in England during its showing at the Royal Academy and at the Brooklyn Museum in the United States. One way to read such acts of violence against the image involves the view that icons in a sense transcend symbolic status and become sentient entities. In this situation, the image, like a bad child, needs to be punished—"I'm going to take that piece of art out behind the woodshed and teach it a lesson." The lesson in question might involve keeping the image from disturbing our aesthetic—and inseparable moral—comfort level. "Sensation" was promoted as putting forth a "totally new and radical attitude to realism. . .a new and radical attitude to life itself." Faced with a perception of social instability, a breakdown of belief in many historical stories and a loss of diverse faiths, numerous individuals at the end of the twentieth century did not want to examine a new and radical attitude toward life. Conversely, they wanted to retreat into a social cocoon of safety (Mitchell, 2000; Steedman, 1998).

Offending images do not interface with the dominant power's machine of forgetting. They bring up issues and concepts that challenge the domination of political, economic, religious, educational and artistic institutions, concerns that those operating in orbit of dominant power would like to see swept under the rug (Hilden, 2000). The aesthetic and thus moral concerns such images raise cannot be separated from individual identities and views of self. In a postmodern society bombarded by visual and print images, saturated by information in a variety of guises and devoid of the ability to make sense of all the babble, the quest for stability of identity intensifies. In the midst of all the changes authoritarian belief structures and fundamentalist religious affiliations proliferate. Numerous individuals seek shelter from the forces of skepticism and indeterminacy, from images that bring such social dislocations into focus.

One of the reasons Karel and I asked our students to read *White Reign* involved the power-related, hyperreal aspects of contemporary identity production. In addition to these more general sociocultural dislocations, many white people in the last decades of the twentieth century and the first decade of the twenty-first century have often found themselves in the throes of an identity crisis. Many conservative whites have maintained that anti-white African Americans and Latinos and radical multiculturalists from all racial backgrounds have conspired to repress the free expression of their white identity. Such a belief generates and intensifies white expressions of anger against nonwhites and creates an atmosphere of racial tension. Such a climate characterized New York City during the "Sensation" exhibit. Unfortunately, the social weather has not changed in the first years of the twenty-first century.

In this identity crisis many white people construct their identity around perceptions of white victimhood. Aaron Gresson (1995) is unambiguous about the white self-portrayal as victim when he writes about the recovery of white domination by the portrayal of blacks and other nonwhites as the new oppressors. In this context whiteness is constructed as a signifier of material deprivation and a litany of present-day grievances. Everyone but white males get advantages, the argument goes, and nonwhites undermine white progress by exploiting white guilt about a long-dead white racism. Such a rhetorical construction, Gresson argues, is a form of vampirism, as whites positioning themselves as victims suck the blood of moral indignation from blacks, Latinos and Native Americans and use it to reposition themselves in the new racial order.

"We" (whites) are victimized by "their" (nonwhites') incompetence, the victimization argument goes, as racial integration has destroyed standards in our schools. Affirmative action, the argument continues, has allowed nonwhite incompetents into our workplaces, undermining the quality of American workmanship. African Americans, Latinos and Native Americans have undermined our family values, bringing the moral tenor of the entire culture down with them. Further, central to the concerns of this chapter, nonwhites are polluting the arts, subverting aesthetic and moral standards in the process. In the U.S. exhibition of "Sensation"—interestingly not the British—African-born Chris Ofili's dung-inscribed "Holy Virgin Mary" was the object of the most condemnation. Mayor Giuliani spoke at length about Ofili's work, virtually ignoring the other art and artists in the exhibition. The mayor's diatribe against Afro-Caribbean artist Renee Cox and her racially explicit "Yo Mama's

Last Supper" in February 2001 was equally readable as a manifestation of the mayor's own white identity crisis.

I will examine this whiteness-oriented dynamic in more detail later in this chapter. Suffice it to say at this juncture that the "offensiveness" of "Sensation" and other artistic productions cannot be understood outside of this racial dimension. White identity concerns in this tense context are often central features shaping designations of offensiveness of *objects d'art* and raising levels of emotional reactions to particular images that seem somehow disproportionate if not inexplicable to observers from other societies. Art museums have traditionally affirmed the histories and aesthetic traditions of the white majority in the United States (Rothfield, 2001). Many such institutions are beginning to understand what may happen when their directors make efforts to appeal to diverse cultural, ethnic and racial communities and include their interests in the operations of the museum. The past fifteen years provide cultural observers with a clearer understanding of the depths of the cultural, ethnic and racial divisions in American society. Indeed, Americans are quite ready to take offense around the intersections of these divisions.

The aesthetic power of a piece of art can increase its social effect, its capacity to elicit emotion, to offend (Leypoldt, 2000). In the cases of Ofili in "Sensation" and Renee Cox in her photograph, "Yo Mama's Last Supper" with her self-portrayal of a nude Jesus at the head of the table, a form of mass iconophobia (Mitchell, 2000) broke out. With Mayor Giuliani provoking it like an adolescent boy cheering an after-school fistfight, the controversy became headline news as it raised ancient questions about the nature and purpose of art. Karel and my students sat in amazement as the "Sensation" controversy brought to public attention the issues we had just introduced in class. Blessed by good timing, we did not have to struggle to convince them that the aesthetic, cultural and political concerns under discussion actually mattered in the world outside our classroom.

Public Consciousness of the Social Role of Art: The Goals of a Progressive Art Education

Studying the public reception of "Sensation" and the politics surrounding it alerts us to the absence of a public conversation about the social role of art. In arguing that American society is not generally aware of the relationships connecting art, politics/power, culture and education, I am not maintaining some hierarchical division between an educated vanguard in the know and the unwashed masses. Such elitism is all too common in high art circles, is offensive and must be avoided by progressive educators and art scholars. Nevertheless, American education, both formal and informal, has never exposed large numbers of individuals to the types of understandings and connections central to this book. Such insights have often been deemed dangerous forms of knowledge and have been banned from the curriculum. Addressing this situation, it may be appropriate to argue that the American public has been victimized and disempowered by a lack of exposure to these issues. Such a lack of experience profoundly shapes the way controversial art such as "Sensation" is publicly received. This lack of awareness must be accounted for as we think about the goals of art education in particular and education in general.

The effort to develop public awareness about these artistic, aesthetic, cultural and political issues is a sensitive pedagogical undertaking. Such concepts do not need to be explained to multiple audiences in the form of an authoritative lecture that designates the "true meaning" of controversial art and the exact nature of the artistic, aesthetic, cultural and political connections previously referenced. A progressive pedagogy that is aware of the complexity of these issues is more concerned with exploring the motivations behind such art, the context from which it emerges, the social forces operating in its orbit, the questions it raises or doesn't raise, its relations to power, the connections between the aesthetic and the political and the social roles it might play. Interpretations and readings need to be offered humbly and always with an appreciation of the many levels of meaning that may emerge when observer encounters artifact (Edelstein, 2000).

Such an approach profoundly differs from the canonical art education that the more privileged members of the culture have traditionally received. Here art is often presented exclusively as high culture or entertainment, designed to fill the cosmos with beauty and refinement. In this articulation the appreciation of art and its goals are the province of a "cultured elite" who possess the cultivated skills and cognitive ability to operate in this rarefied domain. Those of us from "lesser" backgrounds do not possess such training or harbor the necessary ability and thus do not have the capacity to appreciate the finer points of the aesthetic sensibility.

Such elitist orientations help explain why as a society we know so little about art. A central assertion of this work involves the radical belief that most people from any background conceivable can not only understand high canonical art and aesthetics but can understand the unstated cultural assumptions that shape canonical practices while gaining a profound appreciation of multiple ways of viewing and producing art. On this same educational journey individuals can come to understand what official artistic practices tell us about our cultural, political and pedagogical lives and how we are historically shaped creatures who must understand these forces to understand ourselves.

Into this cultural matrix—enter Mayor Rudolph Giuliani stage right. Strategizing for his purported upcoming senate race against Hillary Clinton in 2000, Giuliani understood the artistic/aesthetic consciousness of many New York voters who were affectively and ideologically drawn to him. He was keenly aware of the emotional buttons he could push by speaking out against particular pieces of art and specific images. An excited and energized electorate would be far more likely to go to the polls in the 2000 senatorial election. The "Sensation" exhibit offered a unique opportunity for Giuliani to inspire "his people." No one better understood the magical power of images than the mayor; the connections between art and politics were well known to him.

In numerous interviews I conducted with many students and a few members of the general public—most of whom were culturally and politically conservative—a similar theme emerged in their discussions of "Sensation" and other controversial art. The reason, many maintained, that artists such as Ofili produce offensive images is very simple: They have no talent, and they are trying to get attention for monetary gain. Accompanying this pronouncement, many interviewees spoke of the offensive art as "sick" and "perverted." Giuliani had carefully studied the political consciousness of citizens who expressed these types of perspectives. Politically, it was very much in his interest for citizens to dismiss the artistic and political issues raised by such work as "disgusting" before approaching the ideological dynamics motivating the artist. In this way counterhegemonic, oppositional insights could be kept out of the public conversation and the status quo protected.

By representing transgressive artists as immoral, dirty and sick, Giuliani and other right-wing leaders have successfully precluded any serious public discussion of the discourse, the assumptions and the paradigms of art. A key point in this book involves the assertion that differences between "high art" and "low art" are not permanently etched on the marble tablets of the universe. Instead, such designations are historically constructed and frequently change with the passage of time. Greek tragedies, for example, originally written as plays for popular consumption are now considered high-culture classics (Leypoldt, 2000). I have no doubt that particular works in blues, rock and rap musical genres will eventually be considered high art by many scholarly commentators. Many pieces of so-called "shock art" produced in the last couple decades will migrate to the station of high art. Indeed, such processes have already begun.

In this context, a central dimension of this book emerges: Karel and I are committed to promoting a meta-analysis of the U.S. public's consciousness of art, the nature of its social construction, the cultural and ideological dimensions of this production process and the implications of these complex dynamics for pedagogy. A commitment to such a meta-analysis cannot be secured by merely appealing to First Amendment protections of free expression. A commitment to a serious public conversation about the cultural and political roles of art will be engendered by analysts' ability to explain to various individuals why controversial art is valuable to the social welfare, the health of a democratic society and the vibrancy of a public system of education. This theme runs throughout this work (Leypoldt, 2000; Strauss, 2000).

Making Artistic and Aesthetic Judgments in the Midst of the Culture Wars

It is simply not possible to comment on the social role of art or the worth and meaning of an artistic production without value judgments and specific prejudices. As alluded to above, such judgments and prejudices are constantly shifting as cultural logics and social contexts change. Our perspectives are constantly undergoing challenge and are perpetually "in development." There is little doubt that this book will be viewed differently by readers in 2034 from readers in 2003 or 2004. Indeed, there is little doubt I will, if I am still around in 2034, view it very differently from how I do now. What we are dealing with here is the realm of hermeneutics—another topic to which we will return throughout the book. Involving the art of interpretation, hermeneutics in distinction to the explanatory method of the physical sciences is not grounded on a delineation of causal relations. Hermeneutics is often described as an interaction of horizons, an interaction that takes the form of a dialogue (Berg-Marklund, 1998).

Hermeneutics in an aesthetic/artistic domain asks questions of the meanings of various productions. For example, hermeneutics might ask in reference to Chris Ofili's "Holy Virgin Mary," how do we make the interpretive decision whether elephant dung is a symbol of respect as Ofili told the public repeatedly or a signifier of debasement and perversion as Mayor Giuliani insisted. The study of hermeneutics helps us understand these widely divergent readings of a piece of art, as it focuses our attention on the way context sometimes takes precedence over content in relation to the social, cultural, political and aesthetic concerns of the time period when an object publicly debuts. The context of where and to whom an image might be shown holds profound consequences. The artistic object in question takes on a different meaning when a man asks a woman to "come upstairs and let me show you my erotic etchings" as opposed to when the same erotic etchings are displayed at the Brooklyn Museum.

When hermeneuts ask questions of context in relation to artistic production, interesting things begin to happen. Promoting such questions in teaching and tracing these interesting happenings are key objectives in this book. As we engage in such a hermeneutic process, Karel and I believe that linear chronologies of accepted art history begin to crumble, and ways of seeing and judging particular works of art or groups of artists begin to change. Via the view of a different context, we gain profound new insights into the ways particular cultural networks help shape the production and reception of artistic work. Any mode of assessment involves the construction of hierarchies. This unavoidable process should not be equated with conservative class, racial, paradigmatic, or genre hierarchies grounded on essentialist demarcations of unexamined categorical differences—e.g., high art vs. low art, European "classical" art vs. African "primitive" art (Mitchell, 2000; Duffey, 1996).

We are vitally concerned with these questions of artistic judgment in relation to art from different cultures. By what criteria and on what scale are African or Native American artistic achievements measured? Such a question holds profound implications for understanding the way power operates to shape the way the world and its diverse peoples are viewed, regarded and positioned. When such inquiry is not pursued, art and teaching about art are removed from history, from the experiences of individuals, from the culture in question. Thus, in the analysis of culturally diverse art, we come to understand that even in exhibitions and studies that are on the surface culturally inclusive and celebrations of diversity, cultures can be romanticized, essentialized and frozen in a historical past. Thus, in such interpretive reductionism a new form of "multicultural" ethnocentrism can emerge. Employing the seductive language of multiculturalism and global understanding, Eurocentric categories and modes of judgment continue to dominate the scene. A disturbing European neocolonialism emerges in a pluralist disguise (Hilden, 2000).

Karel's and my own original pedagogical interest in issues of high/low art and good/bad taste cannot be separated from the preceding concepts. In light of such cultural and power-related aspects of artistic judgment, artful teachers become increasingly aware of the insight that distinctions between the classical and the popular, high art and low art cannot be supported on perennial and transcultural aesthetic criteria. We defiantly maintain that popular art can be insightful, inspirational, provocative, intellectually compelling, complex and smart, while high art can be derivative, unimaginative, formulaic, reductionistic and fatuous. As our transgressive hermeneutics exposes the blurred distinctions between high and low art, we are by no means arguing for the dissolution of artistic judgment. Instead, we are calling for a more rigorous form of artistic evaluation that refuses to hide in the facile divisions of art into majestic high art and debased low art.

Indeed, we are issuing a challenge to the art pooh-bahs to come out of their aesthetic cloisters and engage in the difficult act of artistic interpretation in all of its complexity and open-endedness. If the high/low smokescreen is blown away, then new forms of artistic hermeneutics must be devised, new modes of analysis must be debated and hard choices must be made and defended. Our purpose in this context is not to destroy high art but to improve the quality of the aesthetic conversation and extend its themes and concerns to different social domains, to ask questions of the relationship connecting culture and power and to challenge teachers to use the insights that emerge in this process to improve the quality and heighten the ethical awareness of education (Allen, 1995).

In such a reconceptualized artistic context, "popular" can no longer be confused with mediocre nor can European be equated with "classical." As once-intractable boundaries are blurred, new and more rigorous modes of aesthetic evaluation emerge that are grounded on an appreciation of complexity. Such complex aesthetics refuse to simply turn traditional categories on their heads, but work instead to develop more contextualized, theoretically sophisticated and socially aware ways of seeing. In such a new context, an analyst can assert that notoriously inferior productions of popular art can help generate negative cultural and ideological effects without our resorting to aesthetic elitism and categorical authoritarianism (Leypoldt, 2000; Fehr, 1993). The inferior popular art referenced in this context is bad art because of its specific characteristics, not merely because it is popular art. This key distinction is made in this book. In the "culture wars" of the past couple of decades, the distinctions made here are not merely esoteric academic prattle. Indeed, they emerge on this landscape as emotionally charged notions with the power to incite riots and civil unrest in particular venues.

High Anxiety: Conflicting Interpretive Schemata

In chapter 3 "Says Who? Who Decides What Is Art?," I admit my orientation as a culturalist who views art not simply with an eye to the aesthetic but also with an interest in art's relation to culture, cognition, power, history and human possibility. Thus, what you are reading here is a reflection of these concerns and their propensity to highlight the social and political consequences of art and aesthetic issues. With such a disposition in mind, it is a good time to make some personal disclosures: The complex aesthetics I advocate seeks to avoid both some rigid notion of art for exclusively instrumental sociopolitical/cultural outcomes or for purely aesthetic enrichment and pleasure. I am sufficiently hedonistic to enjoy the pleasures art can provide and political enough to seek out art that promotes particular instrumental outcomes in relation to social justice and human development.

Although I am committed to view art as a text for deep reading if not deconstruction, I am not afraid to explore those extratextual and prediscursive dimensions of art and aesthetics and the human experiences they stimulate at the ontological (concerning issues of being) level. Many aspects of artistic/aesthetic experience fall outside the notion of art as text. Without these ontological connections, art would not possess such power to influence the political and cultural realms, to tap into the libidinal energy of human beings and move them in amazingly divergent but highly charged ways. In this context, I have no desire to designate some final resolution of the purpose of artistic/aesthetic experience.

My concern here is to better understand that experience, to make sense of its contemporary influences and the ways it is deployed for particular agendas and to imagine new articulations of artistic/aesthetic purpose in relation to a wide variety of social, cultural, political, cognitive and educational concerns. Aesthetic/artistic understanding will continue to evolve as time passes and contexts change. If we are more acutely aware of its effects and possibilities, we may be better equipped as responsible human beings to produce more significant art, to engage more people in a greater enjoyment of it, to develop more compelling forms of art education and education in general, to use it for more socially just purposes and to connect it to the project of promoting more tantalizing modes of being human. Such goals do not necessitate that we all define art and aesthetics in the same way or ascribe the same frames of reference to our viewing experiences. Indeed, diverse ways of seeing are necessary if we are to continue to learn from the artistic/aesthetic experience. As we assert on numerous occasions in this book, the power of difference, of diverse ways of seeing, is essential to a complex aesthetics, a rigorous education and a healthy democracy.

In contemporary New York City one does not have to look very hard to find diverse ways of seeing art. I interviewed about fifteen conservative Christians and Orthodox Jews, and all held negative views of the exhibit and Ofili's "Holy Virgin Mary" in particular. The responses of conservative Christians about Ofili's work were remarkably similar. In addition to the aforementioned belief that Ofili was an untalented artist seeking attention by producing "dirty pictures," several interviewees spoke of their view of the purpose of art and how "Holy Virgin Mary" related to such a perspective.

Art, they told me, is not merely another form of entertainment for true Christians. Artistic masterpieces help shape us as Christians; they strengthen our faith and our connection to Jesus. Genuine art, they continued, grants us a fleeting view of God and a sense of what heaven will be like. One young woman spoke passionately in this context about "Holy Virgin Mary":

> As true Christians we must always be on guard against representatives of Satan who attempt to confuse us about the role of art. Ofili's Virgin comes from the Devil and tries to pull us away from the path that God has prepared for us. Great art brings us closer to God's grace; that African artist induces us to forsake God. No one who is truly a Christian would portray the Virgin Mary with poop smeared all over her. Christians always have to be on guard against imitation art substituting for the real thing. I'm thankful that the mayor condemned it. Somebody had to do it.

Judging from the wide public support of Giuliani's attack on the Brooklyn Museum, numerous New Yorkers shared the sentiments of the young woman I interviewed. Catholic clergy expressed similar positions during the controversy. Of course, many disagreed as well, but I find it significant that in New York in 1999 and 2000 so many people held such fundamentalist religiously inspired views of the divine role of art.

For many individuals coming from such fundamentalist orientations, our discussion of complex aesthetics and transgressive hermeneutics of art makes little sense. When there is "high divine art" and "low immoral art," complexity is not a concept that holds much significance. Indeed, it can generate much conflict, as it is viewed as a corruption of a sacred canon. Thus, the aesthetic and social roles of art generate as much heat as ever, reflecting and exacerbating divisions within the larger society. In a transgressive hermeneutics of art, analysts agree with the fundamentalists that art has an instrumental value. Of course, the respective nature of such instrumentality is quite different; but, nevertheless, art doesn't simply exist for art's sake in either perspective.

The functional aim or instrumental value of art is rarely conceptualized in total isolation from its aesthetic value regardless of the interpretive schema employed. The practical dynamic of a work of art is often viewed as an aesthetic dynamic in itself, made even more so by its interaction with other aesthetic dimensions of the piece. Thus, the aesthetic and instrumental aspects of art are less at war with one another than they are synergistic, extending the respective power of their different intentions. A piece of art that instrumentally operates to highlight the hidden racism of the New York City schools, for example, does not necessarily find itself aesthetically diminished to a restrictive functionalism (Leypoldt, 2000). Such social and aesthetic judgments must be rendered in relation to the specific work in question.

Other interpretive schemata that might ground a particular hermeneutics of art could include social theorist Julia Kristeva's notion of abjection. Kristeva defines the abject as that which viscerally repulses us, including but not limited to our own mortality, our bodily fluids, and our excrement. Our distress, Kristeva maintains, involves our discomfort with our own physicality and our revulsion with our coexisting cleanliness and uncleanliness. Numerous "Sensation" artists took Kristeva's concern with abjection to heart: Damien Hirst's "A Thousand Years" with its microcosm of flies, maggots, and a cow's head contained in a glass and steel display case; Ron Mueck's effigy of his deceased father, "Dear Dad"; the Chapman brothers' "Great Deeds Against the Dead" with its partially dismembered nude bodies—to name only a few.

In all of these pieces "protective" taboos are broken in a way that forces the viewer to deal with the abject. Only when individuals engage with that which repulses them, Kristeva and the "Sensation" artists maintain, can they begin the process of self-understanding. Thus, in this context, "Sensation" promotes an aesthetic of "exposure therapy" where viewers encounter that which frightens them the most in order to overcome the phobia. Kristeva argues that avant-garde art burns the veil that hides the abject, thus rupturing the power of religious, moral and rationalistic domination (Steedman, 1998). In this interpretive schema, critics such as Mayor Giuliani do not grasp the confrontation with abjection playing out in the exhibition of such work. Their anger is not an unpredictable reaction to a portrayal of realms of human existence that they strive to deny. They object to the abject.

In an era of rationalistic curriculum development, top-down standards, edicts against controversial issues and the deskilling of teachers at all levels of education, teachers need to think carefully about the concepts operating in this conversation about interpretive schemata and offending images. The artful teaching Karel and I are promoting in this book seeks to avoid forms of education that take knowledge for granted, that underestimate the importance of understanding different interpretive schemata in art and all subject matter. Often it is in the controversial areas, in the offending images and ideas, that educators are best able to recognize this importance. That which the dominant culture deems offensive often opens a window to cognitive development, to new levels of insight that produce new modes of consciousness of the way the world operates, the way identity is produced. In this context aesthetic experience can lead to a new level of insight not only about art but about the world at large and ourselves in relation to it. Such an enhanced awareness and the empowerment that can be drawn from it cannot be omitted from a commentary on educational purpose.

Sensational Art in Conservative Times

Controversial or sensational art has traditionally been grounded on an artist's perception of what he or she sees as the pathology of the status quo or the insanity of the dominant culture. As I will discuss in chapter 3, it was well within the tradition of art as social commentary for the French dadaist Marcel Duchamp to display a urinal in an art show in the 1920s. From Duchamp's perspective the world that emerged form the horror of World War I was pathological and insane. Duchamp discerned that he had to use his art to call attention to this reality. Like "shock artists" before and after him, Duchamp railed against the social, cultural, political and religious restrictions that undermine our ability to cope with the derangements that confront us. And like shock artists before and after him, he was reviled by the defenders of the status quo.

One dimension of the tenor of U.S. society at the turn of the twenty-first century, a conservative tone, was reflected by Mayor Giuliani and the reaction to the "Sensation exhibit" and other controversial art in New York City. I was fascinated by the ways New York City newspapers teased the public sensibilities with their coverage of particular pieces of work. Ofili's "Holy Virgin Mary" was consistently described as being "smeared with dung," a phrase guaranteed to rankle conservative readers. When I first saw the painting after having read the description of it in the *New York Times* and the *Daily News*, I was surprised by how inappropriate the application of the verb, smeared, was to this particular painting. Indeed, the Associated Press's headline on the controversy over Renee Cox's "Yo Mama's Last Supper"—"Jesus Is a Woman and She's Naked"—out sensationalized the *National Enquirer*.

In this context it is difficult not to become a little obsessed with the figure of former Mayor Giuliani. His role in these New York art controversies was always central, always designed to elicit particular reactions from diverse members of both New York and U.S. society in general. Portraying himself as a culture cop, the mayor sought to cultivate the image of a brave crusader fighting the lonely battle for decency in a corrupt world. In the years preceding the "Sensation" exhibit, Giuliani sought out transgressive artists, often ordering their arrest and confiscating their art. Indeed, in the first four years of his administration Giuliani ordered over 700 illegal arrests of street artists (Lederman, 1998). In 1998 he created an artist permit that required street artists to gain approval from a mayor-appointed panel before they could show their art on city streets or in its parks. Such repressive actions were grounded on Giuliani's legal notion that visual art is not a—"speech act" and thus does not fall under the umbrella of First Amendment protection.

The requirement for artist permits exists, but there are no restrictions on selling books or newspapers—in Giuliani's legal theory, one is print and is protected, the other is imagery and is not. Of course, Giuliani's interpretation of the First Amendment is not (yet?) dominant, as prevailing legal theory regards images in much the same context as speech (Mitchell, 2000). Some of the mayor's zeal in relation to his tight control of art in the city, many have contended, involved his anger over numerous street artists' display of unflattering political portraits of him in 1997. In February of that year he argued in a brief against street artists claiming First Amendment protection: "An exhibition of painting is not as communicative as speech, literature or live entertainment, and the artists' constitutional interest is thus minimal" (Lederman, 2001).

After the Brooklyn Museum displayed Renee Cox's photograph, "Yo Mama's Last Supper" in an exhibition on African American photography in February 2001, Giuliani promised to appoint a "decency panel" to inspect art that is funded by the city via its support of art museums (Lane, 2001). In April 2001 the twenty-member panel was announced with only one artist chosen to serve on it. The lone artist, Peter Max, declined the appointment when the press confirmed reports he had been convicted of tax evasion. The decency panel reignited the passions of "Sensation" and other art controversies and moved art back to the front pages of New York newspapers. Again "Giuliani versus the art world" became a national story; Jay Leno on the *Tonight Show* referred to the mayor as a fascist. The comedian was not alone as numerous Giuliani-Hitler comparisons erupted around the country. Leno delineated the Führer's effort to rid German museums of what he called degenerate art ("Giuliani Calls for Decency Standard," 2001; "Art vs. Decency," 2001; Edozien, 2001). Art activist Robert Lederman (2001) reminded the readers of his web site of the similarities between Giuliani's and Hitler's positions, as he posted a quotation from *Mein Kampf*:

> Parallel to the training of the body a struggle against the poisoning of the soul must begin. Our whole public life today is like a hothouse for sexual ideas and simulations. Just look at the bill of fare served up in our movies, vaudeville and theaters, and you will hardly be able to deny that this is not the right kind of food, particularly for the youth. . . . Theater, art, literature, cinema, press, poster, and window displays must be cleansed of all manifestations of our rotting world and placed in the service of a moral, political, and cultural idea. (Hitler as quoted by Lederman, 2001)

The debate over controversial art had once again become white hot.

Race as a Central Dimension of Controversial Art: Giuliani and the Crisis of Whiteness

In the New York art controversies of the past few years one can always uncover a racial dimension. At the base of the white victimization impulse discussed previously is a white identity crisis. Mayor Giuliani built his political career around the effort to exploit this crisis; his role in the controversies covered here cannot be understood outside of its conceptual borders. As white people become a minority of the U.S. and New York City populations, many whites have perceived that they are members of a group in crisis and under siege. In this context right-wing spokespeople such as Giuliani seek to position themselves as defenders of beleaguered white people and their sacred contributions in education, religion, literature, history, science and art. As multiculturalists and their African American, Latino, and Native American allies attack these sacred icons, the right-wing argument goes, someone must take a stand, someone must defend the grand accomplishments of white people. Of course, Rudolph Giuliani was ready to play such a role.

In the confused cultural politics of the last decade of the twentieth century, identity politics took on tremendous importance. Many white people in the United States and New York City attempted to deal with the perception that they didn't have an ethnicity or at least didn't have one that was socially validated. Whiteness in this context operated in an identity vacuum that resented those Latino, Asian, African and Caribbean immigrants who entered the country with a clear sense of their ethnic identities. Some progressive whites valued and learned from such immigrants and from permanent nonwhite residents of the country. Such white people would use the cultural knowledge obtained in this context to understand the social and cultural forces that shaped themselves and the world around them. They would come to understand the social role of marginalization in the context of racial and ethnic difference; they would understand the ways such racial/ethnic marginalization was able to muster for a brief period in the last third of the twentieth century a moral and political currency for nonwhite people that could be used to help compensate for their lowly position.

In the crisis of whiteness, it was exactly this moral and political currency that many white people sensed that they didn't possess. Its absence made them profoundly uncomfortable. Many right-wing white political leaders such as Dick and Lynne Cheney, Pat Buchanan, Dick Armey, Jesse Helms, Bob Barr and William Bennett sensed that something was missing in their struggle with the white identity crisis, something very hard to name. Giuliani, maybe better than any other right-wing political leader, understood the kinetic power to be derived from tapping into the white perception of the loss of this moral and political currency. At every juncture of the "Sensation" and Renee Cox art controversies, Giuliani maneuvered to regain this currency for white people.

Giuliani was poised to make use of the obvious demographic changes in the U.S. and in New York City in particular—he reflected the concerns of whites in crisis about the Africanization, Latinization, Asianization and feminization of a white male nation and a white male city (Goldman, 1998). Without ever using white or whiteness as explicit signifiers, Giuliani let his supporters know that "we" could fight off the "corruptions" of the demographic changes and their challenges to "our" institutions. In lieu of the terms *white* or *whiteness*, Giuliani deftly substituted the signifiers, Catholicism, decency, and standards to convey the meaning of whiteness/whites under siege. In this way he could claim the moral and political currency of godliness and decency and depict nonwhites and their "liberal" supporters as immoral agents attempting to attack all that is good about "us." Such tasks could be accomplished while concurrently denying charges of racism or race-baiting.

In the context of whiteness Giuliani used Catholicism and especially anti-Catholicism to hide the racial politics at work. The mayor charged "Sensation" and the "Holy Virgin Mary," in particular, as an overt attack on all Catholics. After the Brooklyn Museum displayed Renee Cox's "Yo Mama's Last Supper," Giuliani characterized the work and the Museum Director Arnold Lehman's willingness to display it as "disgusting and outrageous." The anti-Catholic sentiment displayed by Renee Cox and the Brooklyn Museum, he maintained, has come to be "accepted in our city and our society" (Yuhas, 2001). Working in conjunction with church leaders, Giuliani helped organize white Catholic congregations to call for the closing of the Brooklyn Museum, the slashing of its funding and the resignation of its board members. There was no doubt, Giuliani and numerous white Catholic leaders argued, that Ofili's work was a direct assault on Catholicism. Ofili smeared feces on all that we hold dear. The Brooklyn Museum allowed for the intentional desecration of our most holy saint. What kind of people are these artists and art professionals?

Giuliani's use of decency also helped deflect the racial aspect of the art controversies. Consistently framing the controversies as moral issues, the mayor put together a task force on standards of decency in art after Renee Cox's photograph was exhibited. In this context Giuliani combined the rhetoric of standards with decency for a powerful racial effect. In this discourse who doesn't meet high standards in American social, cultural, educational and moral life? An examination of right-wing language in this context often reveals that it is nonwhites who are positioned as the individuals who have "lowered our standards." It is not unusual that Giuliani resorted to the standards rhetoric after a contentious racial confrontation with Renee Cox over "Yo Mama's Last Supper."

Another feature of Giuliani's effort to subliminally encode the racial dimension of the controversy instead of calling it to overt public attention involved his attack on the "liberal elitism" of the leadership of the New York City art community. While I don't disagree that there are profound elitist elements within the culture of high art, Giuliani's attack seemed revealing in its timing. Museums and their leadership have traditionally operated to affirm the values of dominant culture and the canon of whiteness (Rothfield, 2001). Exhibition managers and educational decision makers in museums have in the past rarely concerned themselves with the perspectives of marginalized individuals and groups within the community. Few complained about the unchallenged elitism of such policies until their exclusive and monocultural nature began to be called into question.

Like the Royal Academy in London, one of the reasons that the Brooklyn Museum chose to display "Sensation" was part of an effort to diversify its collection and the audiences it attracted. There is no doubt that the museums wanted to increase institutional revenues, but there were individuals associated with the museums who authentically wanted to include people from cultural groups long excluded from their activities. The Brooklyn Museum, like many other art museums in urban areas, was following a course of action outlined by the American Association of Museums to reach out to minority communities. It is not serendipitous that Giuliani's attacks on the Brooklyn Museum were issued as it pursued this initiative. The inclusion of controversial, racially inscribed art in a museum conveys a powerful public validation of the art in question (Edelstein, 2000). This certification process bestows a new power and status on not only the work and the artist but on the racial group of which the artist is a member. Such legitimation made many white people in New York City and around the country very angry.

I admit my fascination with Giuliani's role in this controversy as a symbol for an era of the cultural and political life of New York City and the United States in general. He is an icon in the recovery of white supremacy and the racial politics and cultural pedagogies that accompany such a task. After the September 11 attacks on the twin towers, the mayor assumed a national symbolic stature that intersected with these cultural political significations. Giuliani had every right, even a responsibility, to express his perspective about a work of art or an exhibition. Indeed, what a profound pedagogical process Giuliani could have initiated had he chosen to explore the meanings of, say, Ofili's and Cox's work before simply declaring them "disgusting"—he issued such descriptions without even seeing the works. If the mayor had opened and nurtured a public dialogue about these pieces of art and the sociopolitical and pedagogical roles of art in a democratic society, he could have initiated individuals from a variety of backgrounds into an art education that would have served the best interests of the body politic.

In this context, Giuliani could have asked New Yorkers to consider the meaning of the art in question from a number of perspectives (Ross, 2000). He could have explored with, for example, African American citizens the different meanings they ascribed to the works. In this process white citizens could have gained new insights into the social conditions, the emotional hurt and anguish that moved an artist such as Renee Cox to portray Jesus as a naked black woman. What experiences did she and countless other black women endure that would induce them to reflect on the role of the church in a racial and gender context. Listening closely to such viewpoints, many white New Yorkers might have seen "Yo Mama's Last Supper" in a new light, a perspective that could help provide empathy into racial, cultural and ethnic differences and their effects on the city's institutions and everyday life. In such a dialogical context, even phrases such as the crisis of whiteness could have been injected into the public discourse. What a dramatic change in the life of the city such an approach could have catalyzed.

Whiteness, High Art and Standards

But Giuliani didn't open such a dialogue, and the public conversation about art, culture, education, and politics continues to languish in New York City and the nation in general in the first decade of the twenty-first century. A central feature of the artful teaching that Karel and I are advocating here involves recognizing the racial inscriptions on contemporary questions of art, politics and education. In art criticism and pedagogy, this would involve cultivating an awareness of the power and influence of the artistic Eurocenter and in the process promoting other global centers for the production of and ways of viewing art. This is profoundly different from globally expanding the Eurocenter in order to "admit" culturally diverse art into the Eurocanon. When such an expansion occurs, whiteness merely enters a liberal multicultural phase of neocolonialism. The power of whiteness is maintained in a pluralist guise.

A public discussion of the issues raised by controversial art would have exposed the ways the Eurocenter has positioned the art of non-European peoples. African, Asian, Latin American, Native American and other indigenous art has been positioned as primitive, exotic, folkloric and sometimes derivative from European art. European art and culture in general have gained power and identity by juxtaposing themselves against the "undeveloped Third World." As former Secretary of State Henry Kissinger put it in reference to the status of Latin America during a meeting of the Organization of American States in 1969 in Vina del Mar, Chile: "Nothing of importance can come from the South; history is not made in the South" (quoted in Goldman, 1998). Kissinger's statement provides an unguarded insight into a perspective that has dominated U.S. relations with other cultures throughout our nation's history. How ironic it is that in the contemporary New York art controversies in light of centuries of such condescension Chris Ofili and Renee Cox were frequently referred to as the "real racists," the ones who support "bigotry and hatred" toward " a vast majority of the population" (Yuhas, 2001).

Of course, the message implicit in such accusations toward Ofili and Cox was that it is black people who are the real racists in contemporary America and that white people are the victims, the targets of this race hatred. To bring up the history of Western oppression is in the cultural climate of contemporary New York City an act of bigotry. This racial dynamic involves more than what has sometimes been described as a white backlash toward nonwhite demands for equality. What is being referenced here is a new white identity that views all of the advantages in contemporary U.S. society as constructed for nonwhites. We can't teach white history, whites occupying this new white identity point out, but "they" can teach black history all they want. They can have Puerto Rican or African American clubs, but if we try to have all white clubs they call us racists. The absurdity of such representations is quickly exposed when we examine the political economy of whiteness.

Whites, upper and upper-middle class white males in particular, control Western finances, information production, corporate boards, unions, police departments, officer ranks in the military and art museums. White males make up the vast majority of doctors and lawyers and occupy most political offices. There is nothing very complex about these data: White power rules. Even so, despite this obvious circumstance whiteness maintains the power to erase itself—as in the art controversies being examined here. Moreover, in recent years it has gained the ability to portray itself as in a position of victimization by a bigoted cadre of nonwhite and radical multicultural zealots. As the dominant culture, whiteness is capable of sophisticated measures of self-justification that work best when social and economic inequities are hidden from view—inequities from which whites profit unjustly (Merelman, 1986; Fiske, 1994; Jordan, 1995; Nakayama and Krizek, 1995; Rodriguez and Villaverde, 2000).

In art the European, white control of its commerce, historiography and evaluation is merely another dimension of white power erased from the public radar. This power to control the discourse involved with designation of "high art" and "classical art" is expressed in contemporary society as "protecting the last bastions of aesthetic standards" in a world of mediocrity. Chris Ofili and Renee Cox were consistently attacked by defenders of whiteness as "untalented," as "artists intent on destroying aesthetic and moral standards." As commentator Steve Yuhas (2001) wrote about Renee Cox: "The people of New York. . .should refute the anti-Catholic rantings of a naked no talent woman by refusing to pay their admission fee to see her filth." In this defense-of-our-standards rhetoric of whiteness several of the white people I interviewed made numerous references to the distinction between "authentic art" and "hate art" or "junk art." In the context of their comments I interpreted authentic art to signify inclusion in the Eurocanon and hate/junk art to represent a specific form of African American racially inscribed "low art."

These issues are central to the basic concepts of aesthetic judgment, of high and low art, good and bad taste and the purposes of art pedagogy and education in general. They are especially important because such cultural, political and racial concerns are too often dimensions that are excluded from the aesthetic conversation. Even when they are included, concerns with diversity vis-à-vis art are often framed in a rhetoric of multiculturalism that is still inscribed by a Euro-directed universal aesthetic. There is room for art from all racial, ethnic, and cultural backgrounds, the liberal pluralist discourse asserts, but it is always judged in European aesthetic terms. The mode of aesthetic judgment utilized is erased from the light of day and is, therefore, rarely subjected to critical analysis.

Erasing Whiteness from the Canvas: Art as a Racialized Practice

Such an erasure takes place in a fascinating manner that informs the complexity of twenty-first-century racial politics and the way they interface with art and pedagogy. Observing public conversations about cultural aesthetics over the last few years, I have watched white and nonwhite participants promote substantively different viewpoints. Many white spokespeople speak of the basic similarity of the ways culturally and racially different peoples view art. Concurrently, many nonwhite spokespeople emphasize multiple ways of seeing. Advocates of visual similarity often seem rather shocked when Africans, African Americans, Latinos, Native Americans and others point out that the similar way of seeing reflects a universal European aesthetics that masks the presence and power of whiteness (Duffey, 1996; Hilden, 2000).

Many Americans, especially white Americans, are uncomfortable with efforts to address the racialized aspects of everyday life and cultural production in the first decade of the twenty-first century. They are ill at ease with pointing out the racialization of all concepts of universal judgment, often because almost all such proclamations of universalism are white. This is one of many reasons why educators such as Karel and myself are suspicious of standardized curricula, of teaching the "classics," of schools that inculcate "basic knowledge," of art programs that cultivate an appreciation of "great art." We understand that in an era of educational standards opposition to such unexamined designations risks charges of lax scholarship if not ethical or moral relativism. To the contrary, we argue, the ability to recognize difference, to reflect on the criteria used to designate quality in diverse circumstances and traditions is a high-level scholarly, cognitive, political, aesthetic and ethical act.

Of course, this is what artful teaching as we develop it here is all about: engaging students in this rigorous activity in a way that taps into the power of their libidinal energies and connects them to the great human—not simply Western—conversation. As Karel emphasizes throughout the book, this pedagogical goal can be accomplished via the incorporation of art and artistic/aesthetic perspectives in a variety of subjects and curricular contexts. Our caution here is that such artistic and aesthetic work not take place without rigorous analysis of the cultural and racial inscriptions that shape the production and study of art and the political dynamics swirling around the public conversation about and perceptions of the aesthetic domain. Because of these dimensions art, aesthetics, politics, cognition and education cannot be conceptually separated. To be more deeply understood, they must be studied in relation to one another. The weaving of these diverse domains into an interpretive fabric is the intent of this work.

In this integrated interpretive context, for example, it is insufficient to argue that museums and art curriculum developers are now including African, African American and Native American art in the official canon. Haven't curators and scholars over the past few decades removed African and Native American "folk art" from the "otherizing" domain of anthropologists and come to view such art in the way "we" evaluate all art? The question Karel and I would ask in response to such a query is by what (and whose) aesthetic standards do we view all art. Who gets to make the decision? Who chooses what pieces of art represent African and Native American art? Again, I ask "Says Who?" When seen as historicized, enculturated and racialized practices, art and aesthetic judgments upset the apple cart of comfortable white assumptions about the world and its representation.

Walking through the Valley of the Shadow of Death: Challenging the Canon

In the name of social justice, anti-racism, cultural understanding, academic rigor, aesthetic wisdom and cognitive growth, we challenge the European canon of high art. Such a challenge demands that we question accepted modes of aesthetic criticism, problematize the formal criteria used to evaluate artistic quality and seek out diverse schemata of producing and making sense of art. Canonical high art in the West has reflected disturbing Eurocentric biases. As a supremist orientation that corrupts social perceptions while disguising itself as universalist, Eurocentrism stands for civilization, high standards and the defense of classical cultural production. Our challenge to Eurocentrism is based on the belief that art and pedagogy function at their best when they generate compelling responses from those who come into contact with them, expose individuals to ways of seeing they have never encountered, confront an unjust status quo, and initiate democratic social change (Giuffre, 1997; May, 1999).

As Karel and I were developing our course, "High and Low Art: Good and Bad Taste," we anticipated the emergence of these canonical challenges. We knew that we would ask our students to understand and deal with such inquiries and that we would obtain diverse student responses to them. Questions about Eurocentrism inevitably infiltrate any rigorous analysis of issues of high/low art and good/bad taste. Indeed, if we listen to diverse artistic commentators from both within Western societies and around the globe, it is hard to exclude them at the beginning of the twenty-first century. Our point in the course was and our point in this book is not some sophomoric attack on anything labeled high art, not at all. Our purpose, our careful walk through the valley of the shadow of death, involves the interrogation of a Eurocentric canon deemed high art and the elitist, narrow, parochial and exclusionary criteria used to validate aesthetic worth.

We would have hoped (probably naively) that former Mayor Giuliani could have adopted a similar questioning approach to the artistic, aesthetic and cultural issues raised by "Sensation" and Renee Cox instead of immediately locking into his rottweileresque attack mode. Baring his teeth, the mayor forewent any attempt to open a dialogue between contentious communities; instead he pushed them farther apart. Circling the wagons against any canonical questioning, Giuliani and the conservative defenders of the canon precluded any public discussion of the racialized practices so central to the history of Western art in general and the New

York "dirty art" controversies in particular. Wouldn't a canonical challenge be valuable that questioned, for example, the racialized practice of the Smithsonian Institution and the Heye Center's maintaining a collection of Native American art, artifacts, and "human remains"—20,000 American Indian skeletons (Leypoldt, 2000; Ross, 2000; Hilden, 2000).

What messages are transmitted by high-art institutions keeping the remains of Native American ancestors in their storage rooms? Is this an artistic, cultural, and political issue that needs to be examined by students and citizens in a variety of pedagogical contexts? Does knowledge of such realities open up the possibility of cultural explorations that help sensitize us to issues of race, ethnicity and power? Our challenge to the canon asks these types of questions. It alerts Americans and others to the historical presence of racism and ethnic bias referenced in the shock art that often offends particular sensibilities. The art that Giuliani so vehemently condemned, for example, cannot be understood without an awareness of the dehumanizing social forces that engaged the artists' imagination and motivated the production of particular works. At the initial conception of such art, a social injury could be identified (Allen, 1995; Mitchell, 2000). Our canonical challenge exposes these dynamics.

In a context of white crisis and white victimization, our call for an analysis of the dehumanizing social forces referenced in particular controversial works often falls on angry ears. Writing on "Yo Mama's Last Supper" for the newspaper *The Delta Collegiate Online*, Gary White (2001) expresses the anger many conservative whites display toward canonical challenges referencing race:

> The last issue with this piece is one that I can't really excuse. Why is Judas portrayed as white? This really makes me mad. If it was in reverse and Judas was the single African American in the piece, the Brooklyn Museum of Art would have never had the gall to display it. Not only this but the artist of such a piece would have most likely been ostracized from the arts community. Perhaps Cox was just afraid to portray African Americans in a negative light. If that was the case I think it's just as sad that people cannot come to terms with the idea that there are good and bad people of every color. It makes me wonder what Cox thinks of Jesse Jackson paying off his mistress with charity dollars.

As African Americans and other groups marginalized around the axes of race, class, gender and sexuality have struggled for social justice, they have produced art designed to reflect and further the cause. As more and more such works have found their way into mainstream institutions, conservatives grew increasingly upset by the alternative and unsettling views of the world they generated. As conservatives have made their abandonment-of-standards argument in reference to the inclusion of such work in hallowed museums, the degree of ethnocentrism and elitism associated with the high-art canon has become more and more clear. High art was not only the province of one cultural tradition, but the capacity to produce and appreciate it lay beyond the cognitive abilities of common people. A shadow of death actually follows such perspectives and shades the exclusionary practices that emerge from the conceptual cocoon they weave. "We don't want politicized art in our museums," the guardians of the canon broadcast, "we want high-quality art." In this context a strict distinction is constructed between "neutral" and "political" art (Giuffre, 1997; Rothfield, 2001; Allen, 1995; "Lecture on Censorship and the Arts," 2000).

From the beginning of efforts to bring diverse works into high-status museums, conservatives deployed the attack on so-called politicized art. When the Metropolitan Museum exhibited the innovative "Harlem on My Mind" in the 1960s, right-wing detractors proclaimed that there was "no art" in the entire collection. All "Harlem on My Mind" represented, they contended, was a politicization of the Met. The same arguments were used over the following decades, and by the late 1980s conservatives appeared ready to eliminate museums in order to neutralize the canonical challenges of political art (Rothfield, 2001). The inseparability of "racial" from the "political" signifier in conservative discourse is evident in most of these art wars. Whites are under siege the conservatives maintained, using a wide variety of rhetorical cloaking devices. And now "they" want to attack "our" art canon, a body of work that stands as the last bulwark against the erosion of aesthetic standards.

Artful Teaching, Art and Educational Purpose: Just What Are We Trying to Do?

As we analyze the connections that conceptually bring together high and low art, good and bad taste, aesthetic criticism, cultural conflict, the politics of art, offending images and cognition, we are constantly monitoring the implications of these complex interactions in the context of artful teaching and educational purpose. The nature of the public conversation and the political dynamics that surrounded "Sensation" and Renee Cox provide insight into the status of education in the first decade of the twenty-first century. A familiarity with a multiperspectival discourse of art and aesthetics provides new lenses through which to consider educational purpose in a democratic society. Implicit in our notion of artful teaching is a rejection of the mainstream view of schooling and education as an adjustment to the status quo, training for entry into the corporate structure and a preparation for individual socioeconomic mobility (Boggs, 2000). Understanding that schooling has historically served as a mechanism for social regulation (Allison, 1995), we operate to devise alternative purposes for the contemporary educational process.

In this context artful teaching is always aware that schooling and the education that takes place in the society at large—a.k.a. cultural pedagogy—is not simply an academic process but a political process as well. Education by nature is a political act. This is not an easy notion to sell, as students and people living in the United States in general acquire early in their lives the ideological notion that education is a neutral process. A quick historical overview of American schooling quickly dispels this notion. Studying this educational history throughout my career, I have come to the conclusion that schooling has been employed not as much to foster democracy as to promote the social regulation of particular individuals.

Indeed, in the attempt to produce suitable citizens and safe workers, political and educational leaders have rarely questioned the justice of the existing sociopolitical order; moreover, they have rarely supported attempts to produce a curriculum that rigorously examines power inequalities and different forms of oppression. Western democracies are presented to students as places where a legal equality of opportunity has been achieved. In such a context why would mainstream educators waste their time dealing with the blather of progressives concerned with power, knowledge production, democracy and race, class and gender relations? Of course, the answer artful teachers provide to such a question is that they don't. If inequality and domination do not exist, then why do artful teachers need to examine the way such forces shape institutions, produce particular curricula, and construct the lives of individuals (Carlson, 1991, 1997; Horn, 2000; McLaren, 2000; Hinchey, 1998; Soto, 2000; Steinberg, 2001)?

Defenders of the canon, of unexamined categories of high art, do not promote a cultural pedagogy but a "cultured" pedagogy. A cultural pedagogy examines the complexity of knowledge production, power relations and the ways these dynamics construct consciousness and identity in everyday life. A conservatively inscribed cultured pedagogy is designed to provide students with an encounter with high culture. Through exposure to the high art, great literature, and the classics of the Eurocanon, individuals can gain socioeconomic mobility and become "cultured." "Do not challenge us," canonical proponents demand, "just allow high culture to work its aesthetic magic." "The low art of popular culture debases our people," the defenders maintain. The purpose of schooling is to point out the aesthetic poverty of such popular experiences and replace them with "the best human beings have created."

Of course, in response to such claims Karel and I quickly assert that the definition of "the best that human beings have created" in the canonical tradition is always European and mostly male; such cultural production reflects only one of many cultural traditions' attempts to make sense of the world. It is not a sufficiently rigorous and comprehensive approach to education in a globalized and multicultural world. The individuals such an education produces do not have enough experiences with difference to reflect on the parochialism that often plagues Western art and aesthetics, knowledge production, politics, cognitive studies, and education. We can do better; we can create an education, an artful teaching that helps us situate ourselves in the world around us, in the cultural traditions that have much to teach us about human experience if we would only listen.

Such issues raise the most basic questions about the purpose of education. In art education or in any academic discipline is the purpose of pedagogy to merely pass along the verified truths of the dominant culture? Is there a more complex role for education in a democratic society? Might one of the purposes of education in democracy involve raising questions about the consistency of our collective and individual actions in relation to democratic and egalitarian principles? Is it possible that a society is democratic to the degree that it allows for and encourages self-criticism and self-reflection in conjunction with its efforts to improve itself through careful attention to the wisdom of others? Such difficult questions seem somewhat irrelevant as I examine the teaching of art and art history in numerous educational settings. In many locations artistic, aesthetic, and art historical study involves little more than the memorization of particular names, dates, and events—an unreflective litany of monocultural milestones (Allen, 1995).

The artful teaching promoted here is democratic, critical and rigorous, as it maneuvers through pedagogical minefields of unexamined knowledge. Refusing to take certified information on art, science, history, politics or cognition for granted, our artful teaching knows that reductionistic canonical transmission subverts the rigor of the cognitive process, the disposition to learn and the quality of education in general. When dominant transmission models of education demand that students passively absorb "truths" from canonical cold storage, knowledge is removed from the contextual forces that helped produce it, shape it and certify it (Berg-Marklund, 1998; Boggs, 2000).

Obviously, a key goal of this book involves describing and providing examples of these contextual forces as they construct the knowledge produced about art and aesthetics and the pedagogical processes that engage such information. What we are dealing with in this context are epistemological questions about art and education. Such epistemological questions induce artful teachers to gain a more sophisticated understanding of the complexities of the knowledge produced about art while concurrently assessing the pedagogical consequences of such a process. With these concepts in mind, artful teachers are empowered to examine their personal relationship to this epistemology of art and to develop curricula that reflect their understanding of the politics of the canon, the potential benefits of artistic/aesthetic analysis and the purposes of education.

At Their Best Art and Education Raise Questions in the Public Mind: Upgrading the Conversation

Students who are aware of the complex debates about knowledge production and aesthetic evaluation in the discipline of art will not only be more cognitively sophisticated but will be more motivated to continue studying such issues. They will find the matrix of political and cultural conflicts hidden in the art canon more challenging and interesting than the reductionistic transmission pedagogies they had in all probability encountered previously. Art and education operate most successfully when they engage their audiences in the particularities of the power struggles that have constructed them as institutions. The worlds of art and education did not immaculately come into being in their present forms. The state of contemporary art and education is the result of a long series of conflicts, contentions and power plays that moved the institutions in particular directions. The exposure and study of these processes promote thought and conversation; such analysis when shared with the public provokes questions previously not considered by most people.

One of our goals in this book is to engage the public in such inquiries and conversations. In my conversations with students and members of the general public from New York since the beginning of the "Sensation" controversy in the fall of 1999, I have found individuals who are not conversant with the social and cultural roles played by art. The notion that art might assume a political role or be a force in promoting social change seemed particularly foreign to my interviewees. When I asked if art had ever moved them to reconsider particular beliefs, I was often met with incredulity:

> "Mary": I don't think about things like that. My parents didn't raise us that way. We were taught to work hard and keep our feet on the ground. My boyfriend does some drawing, but his pictures don't make me think about my beliefs. I'm not sure what you want me to say.
>
> JLK: When you look at your boyfriend's pictures, what do you think about?
>
> "Mary": I don't know [laughs]. I just think about how much they look like his car, I guess.
>
> JLK: Did you ever take an art class in high school or when you were an undergraduate in college?
>
> "Mary": Yes, one in high school and one in college.
>
> JLK: Did you ever discuss what the artist was trying to evoke in the mind of the viewer? In your mind?
>
> "Mary": Yeah, but it didn't have anything to do with my beliefs or stuff like that.
>
> JLK: What did it have to do with?
>
> "Mary": Beauty.
>
> JLK: Maybe my question is not clear. When I say, beliefs, I'm referring to the ways you thought about yourself, the ways you viewed the world, the ways you thought about other groups of people. Did the art you saw in class move you to think about these types of things?
>
> "Mary": Yes, that's more clear. Now I think I know what you want. I understood there was beauty in a lot of places you might not think of at first. I thought deeper about beauty.

In my conversations with "Mary" and others, I pushed them to contemplate art's connections with other domains. Even though all of them were college graduates, and most had taken art courses in both high school and college, virtually none of them revealed any exposure to or familiarity with the social, cultural or political roles of art. From my interviewees I gained the sense that they tacitly believed—though none overtly stated it—that the role of art was limited to the aesthetic dimension and the meaning of art was self-contained. Artistic meanings were beyond subjective interpretation and were timeless and intractable. When asked what a piece of art meant, most believed there was an objective, correct answer to such an inquiry. The role of the educated viewer in this context was to learn the correct interpretation and file it away for future reference if the work was ever encountered again. The role of art education was to pass these "answers" along to students. The main question my subjects' art education had raised for them involved: "Oh, we studied that painting. What did it mean?"

Questions concerning the rules of artistic/aesthetic evaluations or canonical challenges were not a part of my interviewees' conceptual universe. Questions concerning the distinctions between high art and low art in the educational cosmos they had visited were blasphemous; inquiries into the multivalent relationships between art and real people and their everyday lives were viewed by the canonical educators who taught my interviewees as "off the subject," a diversion from the goal of acquainting students with as much great art as they could handle. Karel's and my concerns with questioning artistic/aesthetic paradigms, examining discursive practices, exposing hidden assumptions and analyzing racial inscriptions would have been viewed as dangerous ideas and poisonous diversions in the march toward a cultured pedagogy of art.

Raising such questions and engaging in such analysis in art reflect the larger goals of artful teaching. In this pedagogical context students gain the ability and the disposition to attend to the visual and linguistic texts that surround them. To begin this process teachers engage students in analyzing the texts that they encounter in their daily lives. In this context students learn analytical skills and research abilities that connect their everyday experiences in the world to academic knowledge and scholarly expertise. What we are dealing with here is the development of critical viewing skills that help students make sense of various knowledge forms from art, media imagery, iconographs and techniques of political persuasion to traditional literature.

Using lessons from various paradigms and cultural forms of artistic analysis, artful teachers help themselves and their students develop new ways of reading the world. In this context they are able to transcend the monologic of one-truth ways of seeing that privilege one culture's way of making meaning. Escaping such reductionism they pursue new frames of reference that open new insights into the forces that shape their lives. Such understanding helps teachers and students use art to better appreciate the cultural texts that surround them while at the same time creating new identifications with and attention to art. This expanding synergy operates at the core of artful teaching. In this manner we avoid a view of art as only some narrow and exclusive search for beauty that causes us to miss more slippery features of the *Zeitgeist* surrounding us (Allen, 1995; Steedman, 1998).

As previously asserted, by no means do we dismiss beauty or the pleasure of artistic encounters but connect them to our pedagogical and cognitive concerns with enhanced awareness and a passionate disposition toward learning. This is the context in which we begin to grasp concepts and issues that we had never before contemplated. Artful teachers and their students begin an intellectual journey that explores the ways meaning is made, consciousness is constructed and social, cultural and political change occurs (Leypoldt, 2000; May, 1999). This is a profoundly different process of education from the transference of predigested data that now occurs in technical standards-driven education. The struggle for artistic freedom parallels the struggle for a rigorous and intellectually free education. Such an intellectual freedom involves the rights of artful teachers and their students to derive their own meanings and interpretations of the knowledge of academic disciplines while contributing to the production of such data. It involves allowing them to travel wherever their curiosity and passionate disposition toward learning takes them.

Artful Teaching and Educational Purposes: Connecting Students to and Changing the World

Amidst all of the interpretive and analytical complexity swirling around artful teaching, there exists a rather simple objective that moves our actions: Artful teaching seeks to connect teachers and students to the world so they can better understand it, view themselves in relation to it and change it in a democratic and egalitarian manner. In this context artful teachers encourage skepticism about the "official story," the "correct meaning" of an artifact or a piece of art and seek diverse perspectives on a variety of topics. Always treasuring curiosity, artful teachers seek to turn out learners committed to a life of learning. Seeing the world as a classroom, such students connect social, cultural, aesthetic, scientific, literary, historical, political and economic knowledge to 'community-building activities. As educator Grace Lee Boggs (2000) puts it:

> Classes of school children from K-12 should be taking responsibility for maintaining neighborhood streets, planting community gardens, recycling waste, rehabbing houses, creating healthier school lunches, visiting and doing errands for the elderly, organizing neighborhood festivals, painting public murals. The possibilities are endless. This is the fastest way to motivate all our children to learn and at the same time reverse the physical deterioration of our neighborhoods. It is a wonderful way to nurture the desire of children to be of service and provide opportunities for children to make a difference and win the respect of their peers and elders.

There is a tendency in modernist European thought and the pedagogy it supports to devalue the importance of everyday life, the lived world of individuals. The purpose of education in this modernist context is simply to pass along a body of fixed texts that have become sacred icons with fixed meanings. The insight that culture is created in interactions between individuals, in debates, conflicts, negotiations, compromises and agreements, helps us derive meaning from the social texts and the knowledge a group of people produces. Viewing the "Sensation" exhibit or Renee Cox's work without an understanding of Mayor Giuliani's fights with particular elements within New York City and beyond, without an appreciation of the boiling racial tensions in the city and without a knowledge of the crisis of whiteness vis-à-vis the historical context of the last decades of the twentieth century would leave us with a very shallow appreciation of the multiple layers of meanings operating in and around such works of art. At the same time, studying these particular works of art and the cultural dynamics surrounding them grants us not only a deeper insight into American society at the beginning of the twenty-first century but a new context from which to view ourselves and our relationship to that society.

In the modernist pedagogical devaluation of everyday life, the fixed texts that are to be committed to memory are so far removed from the lived worlds of students that curiosity is quickly eradicated. As I study the educational standards movement that has swept the United States over the past decade (Horn and Kincheloe, 2001; Kincheloe and Weil, 2001), I have observed the hyperextension of this tendency. Students are often subjected to meaningless memorization drills on canonical material that holds no meaning for them on any level other than its use on multiple-choice standards tests. Every morsel of data stands alone, isolated from history, from the social dynamics that grant it meaning, from any connection to anything that remotely matters to students.

Teacher: The next slide, class, is Pablo Picasso's "Guernica." It was painted in 1937 and it is about war.

Student 1: How do you spell "Guernica"?

Teacher: G-u-e-r-n-i-c-a. Did everyone get that?

Student 2: What war is it about?

Teacher: I'm not sure. Just remember on the test that it's about war; that'll be enough. Everyone have that? Let's go on to the next slide, we have a lot to cover.

The irrationality in the name of rationality of such disconnected teaching is palpable. Teachers are placed in horrible situations, as they are often evaluated in respect to how well students score on standards tests. Teachers who teach with respect to both the scholarly process and the engagement of students in the analysis of the significance of curricular content in their lives—modest educational goals, I admit—often have to accomplish such tasks in secret acts of curricular subversion. Artful teachers recognize these irrationalities, as they seek to connect students with the romance of learning. To accomplish such tasks, these teachers research the lives of their students so as to better connect their lessons to student experience. Artful teachers become life historians of their students, exploring their fears and dreams, their places in the social hierarchy, their romantic relationships, their vocational aspirations and their relationships with teachers.

As teachers who are researchers, artful teachers develop a double consciousness that is aware of the construction of disciplinary knowledge along with its exclusions and the production of their students' consciousnesses and identities. In this way they massage the curriculum, problematize it, develop multiple ways of connecting it to what they know about their students and the communities in which they live. Artful teachers work hard to develop this double consciousness and to reveal the social, scientific, political, cultural and educational forces that impede their own and their students' achievement of it. Indeed, in many contemporary educational settings, teachers are taught not to develop such a "dangerous" double consciousness, not to analyze the existing goals of education or prescribed modes of teaching within a broader social, cultural, aesthetic and political context. In this way the origins and effects of regressive educational policies are hidden from the light of day. "Guernica," after all, is about war.

Artful teaching with its rigorous notion of scholarship, its teachers as researchers, its dedication to connecting the curriculum and students to the lived world sees itself as a form of citizenship education. As such, students never separate rigorous scholarly analysis from the ways such skills can be used in the public space of democracy and self-government. Teachers and students, for example, who understand the layers of sociocultural, political, aesthetic and pedagogical complexity surrounding the art controversies we foreground in this book are better equipped to participate in public conversations and political debate. They are better prepared to control their own lives and enter into community empowerment projects. In much that passes for high-standards education in the first decade of the twenty-first century, these civic concerns are irrelevant.

The essential scholarly and democratic task of questioning accepted assumptions or shaking up comfortable beliefs is regarded in many contemporary schools and educational systems as an act of treason (Warner, 1999). Artful teaching is horrified by such anti-democratic ideology and seeks to confront it wherever it presents itself. As Paulo Freire argued throughout his life, democratic educators have a moral responsibility to challenge oppressive agents and to work for socially just change. In an era marked by the censorship of art, an insidious racism and anti-democratic, unchallengable public school pedagogies, the need for the critical eye of artful teaching is greater than ever. This book is dedicated to confronting these interacting travesties.

References

Allen, G. (1995). Cultural studies in the undergraduate program: Pedagogical renaissance or curriculum life? <http://www.towson.edu/~sallen/CLST/lecture.html>.

Allison, C. (1995). *Present and past: Essays for teachers in the history of education.* New York: Peter Lang.

Art vs. decency. (2001). http://www.greenspun.com/bboard/q-and-a-fetch.msg.te?msg-id+004cza

Berg-Marklund, M. (1998). Pictures give us a visual manifestation of intuitive thinking. http://ww.skolor.lund.se/tuna/IT/knost/english/maria/m-engl.htm

Boggs, G. (March 23, 2000). Children's miracle needed to solve school crisis. Paper presented to *Voices in Dialogue Series*, Philadelphia School District. <http://www.boggs-center.org/phil3-23-00.htm>

Bratten, J. (1996). Wherefore fine arts? *The University Concourse*, 1, <http://www.theuniversityconcourse.com/1.2.2-27-1996/bratten.htm>

Carlson, D. (1991). Alternative discourses in multicultural education: Towards a critical reconstruction of a curricular field. Paper presented to the Bergamo Conference on Curriculum Theory and Classroom Practice, Dayton, Ohio.

Carlson, D. (1997). *Making progress: Education and culture in new times*. New York: Teachers College Press.

Clark, T. (1997). *Art and propaganda in the twentieth century: The political image in the age of mass culture*. New York: Harry Abrams.

Duffey, A. (1996). Art history in South Africa: Past and present. Paper presented at the 29th International Congress of the History of Art, Amsterdam.

DuGay, P., Hall,S., Janes, L., MacKay, H., Negus K. (1997). *Doing cultural studies: The story of the Sony Walkman*. London: Sage.

Edelstein, T. (2000). Sensational or status quo? Museums and public perception. Paper presented at the Cultural Policy Program at the University of Chicago.

Edozien. F. (April 7, 2001). Leno ripped for fascist jab at Rudy. *New York Post*, p. 2.

Fehr, D. (1993). *Dogs playing cards: Powerbrokers of prejudice in education, art, and culture*. New York: Peter Lang.

Fiske, J. (1994). Audiencing: Cultural practice and cultural studies. In N. Denzin and Y. Lincoln (Eds.), *Handbook of Qualitative Research*. Thousand Oaks, CA: Sage.

Free expression (October 24, 2000). <www.delawareonline.com/newsjournal/opinion/view/02182001.html>

Giuffre, K. (1997). Uncircled wagons: Art world fragmentation and NEA reauthorization. <http://www.frostburg.edu/dept/soci/rmoore/article3.htm>

Giuliani calls for "decency standard" to tame outrageous artwork. (2001, February 16). <http://www.pipedream.nu/010216/news/n13.html>

Goldman, S. (1998). The Latin Americanization of the United States. *Art Nexus*, 29, pp. 80–84.

Gresson, A. (1995). *The recovery of race in America*. Minneapolis: University of Minnesota Press.

Gresson, A. (2002). *America's atonement*. New York: Peter Lang.

Hilden, P. (2000). Race for sale: Narrative of possession in two "ethnic" museums. *The Drama Review*, *44*, p. 3.

Hinchey, P. (1998). *Finding freedom in the classroom: A practical introduction to critical theory*. New York: Peter Lang.

Horn, R. (2000). *Teacher talk: A postformal inquiry into educational change*. New York: Peter Lang.

Horn, R. & Kincheloe, J. (2001). (Eds.). *American standards: Quality education in a complex world—The Texas case*. New York: Peter Lang.

Housman, N. (1999). On the fast track to fairness in education. <http://www.emary.edu/womens_center/housemmanfl.html>

Jordan, J. (1995). In the land of white supremacy. In C. Berlet (Ed.), *Eyes right: Challenging the right-wing backlash*. Boston: South End Press.

Kincheloe, J. & Weil, D. (2001). (Eds.). *Schooling and standards: An encyclopedia*. Santa Barbara, California: ABC-Clio.

Kincheloe, J., Steinberg, S., Rodriguez, N., & Chennault, R. (1998). (Eds.). *White reign: Deploying whiteness in America*. New York: St. Martin's Press.

Lane, J. (2001, April 6). Untitled. <http://users.1st.net/jimlane/2001arch/4-6-01.html>

Lecture on censorship and the arts. (2000). <http://www.samuseum.org/oct2000/censorship.html>

Lederman, R. (1998). Giuliani's New Year's gift to street artists. <http://www.infoshop.org/nyork/street_artists.html>

Lederman, R. (1999). Giuliani: Art critic. <http://www.infoshop.org/nyork/art1.htm.>

Lederman, R. (2001, April 23). Giuliani issues new statement on artist's free speech. <http://www.baltech.org/lederman/giuliani-statement-4-23-01.html>

Leypoldt, G. (2000). The pragmatist aesthetics of Richard Shusterman: A conversation. *Zeitschrift für Anglistik und Amerikanistik: A Quarterly of Language, Literature and Culture, 48*, 1, pp. 57–71.

May, L. (1999). When art shocks. <http://infoculture.cbc.ca/archives/visart/visart.10271999monstrance.phtm.>

McLaren, P. (2000). *Che Guevara, Paulo Freire, and the pedagogy of revolution*. Lanham, MD: Roweman and Littlefield.

Merelman, R. (1986). Domination, self-justification, and self-doubt: Some social-psychological consideration. *Journal of Politics, 48*, pp. 276–299.

Mitchell, W. (2000). Offending images. Paper presented at the Cultural Policy Program at the University of Chicago.

Nakayama, T., & Krizek, R. (1995). Whiteness: A strategic rhetoric. *Quarterly Journal of Speech, 81*, pp. 291-309.

Pheonix6926. (2000). The censorship of art. *Planet Papers*. <http://www.planetpapers.com/asserts/2046.html>

Rodriguez, N., & Villaverde, L. (2000). *Dismantling white privilege: Pedagogy, politics, and whiteness*. New York: Peter Lang.

Ross, D. (2000). An all too predictable sensation. Paper presented to the Cultural Policy Program at the University of Chicago.

Rothfield, L. (2001). Introduction: The interests in "Sensation." *Unsettling sensation: Arts policy lessons from the Brooklyn Museum of Art controversy*. New Brunswick, NJ: Rutgers University Press.

Sanders, R. (1999). The best show in town: Art vs. politics. *US Africa Online*. <http://.www.safricaonline.com/sandersart1099.htm.>

Soto, L. (2000). (Ed.). *The politics of early childhood education*. New York: Peter Lang.

Steedman, A. (1998). Selling the ugly. <http://www.alexei.ic24.net.html.shockart.html>

Steinberg, S. (2001). (Ed.). *Multi/intercultural conversations: A reader*. New York: Peter Lang.

Strauss, D. (2000). The false promise of the First Amendment. Paper presented to the Cultural Policy Program at the University of Chicago.

Warner, C. (1999). Opinions of administrators, faculty, and students regarding academic freedom and student artistic expression. Doctoral Dissertation, College of Education, Virginia Tech University.

White, G. (2001, March 29). The art of censorship. *The Delta Collegiate Online*. http://www.delta.edu/~colpaper/2001/3-29-01/artofcensorship.html

Yuhas, S. (2001). Artistic differences—Anti-religious photograph fires up New York mayor. <http:www.steveyuhas.com>

TWO

Art and the Education of Artful Teachers

Karel Rose

In the aftermath of the horrific attacks on the World Trade Center and the Pentagon, our ideas about a free society are being challenged in ways that are unprecedented in our history. More than buildings are imploding; our conceptual frameworks are fracturing. We are suddenly required to articulate and act on our priorities. Understandably, many will call for a hard-line, purely intellectual solution to this unspeakable atrocity as if the road to what is good and just is unambiguous. But feelings and personal convictions will always interfere no matter how horrific the situation. Consumed by a sense of helplessness and fear for ourselves and future generations, many will say that this is not the time for personal expression and the arts. But how does one disengage with a way of knowing and being in the world? Over the centuries, it is the arts that have provided people with the courage to understand the historical moment. So it has been. Grief, terror, even armageddons inspire the artistic sensibility and offer a way of coping. Expressiveness has always been a necessary buffer in the face of horror. In concentration camps, in prison cells, at funerals, the transformation of grief and rage into art has been a survival strategy for making sense of the senseless. To suggest that there is no room for art in our lives at this time is to understand art as a voyeuristic, frivolous activity rather than a significant avenue for understanding. Words, music, dance and images are powerful determinants of what we think, and that is why they must be used with care and not be trivialized.

Once again, teachers will find themselves on the front line. As the storytellers of the culture, their art brings meaning to the world for their students. Teaching is a drama constructed in a given space and time. One way to position the agony of the terrorist attack is through a greater interconnectedness with other cultures and diverse ways of thinking. Clearly, this does not mean accepting terrorism. Both teachers and their students need to ask significant philosophical questions about existence, knowledge and values. Within the framework of our belief systems, the events of September 11, 2001, require a search for a holistic worldview that does not reduce knowledge to any one perspective, whether it be spiritual, economic, scientific, aesthetic or historical. A parochial vision with its exclusive focus on local and Western ideologies is proving to be destructive to those very values of democracy and justice that have been so shockingly transgressed. The making of meaning in our complex world needs to be built on a greater acknowledgment of diversity. The arts with their broad spectrum can help us to understand this aspect of our dilemma. The offensive against those who have violated basic human rights will have to proceed on many fronts, but our revulsion with the ghastly will greatly influence our behavior. Shocked into living with new ambiguities, postmodernism, culturalism and the aesthetic way of knowing will have to articulate their principles with even greater clarity. Teachers will have to be taught and teach that wholeness, context and connectedness are more than reading strategies. They are metaphors for living a transformed world that has relied too heavily on smoke and mirrors.

The artist, like the mischievous child in school, often finds himself in the principal's office getting into trouble with society's bosses. The behavior of the child and the artist may be misconstrued and severely punished when a prevailing hierarchy is threatened. Salman Rushdie gets death threats from the ayatolla, Oriana Fallaci remains in hiding, a controversial exhibit at the Brooklyn Museum of Art brings a police presence and a white teacher who reads *Nappy Hair* to her class is suspended. What to read, what to view, whom to love and whom to hate is prescribed by most religious, cultural and political groups with the recognition that the arts and education can present powerful challenges to their status quo. As expressive modes, the arts resist zip-coding and challenge extant givens. Even so, how can artists and teachers whose work it is to re-present the world do anything else? We are by nature meddlesome, playful and inquisitive. Inquiry does not require that we throw the baby out with the bath water only that we consider alternate ways of bathing the baby. For history has shown that when knowledge flourishes in a free society, many prevailing notions are reaffirmed.

Though education is acknowledged as critical for human growth and will happen with or without formal schooling, art is not always recognized as central to the process. Yet take a closer look. Art is omnipresent. It is in our homes, on our tables, at our ceremonies, on our bodies and on our streets. The "dailiness" of our lives is enlivened by the presence of art. Our ancestors would be surprised to discover that their decorated water jugs, cave paintings and stories are now termed "art" and are in glass cases in museums. Nevertheless, despite a growing number of studies which firmly acknowledge the arts as critical for education, there is still considerable resistance to giving aesthetic experiences a central place in the classroom.

In an era when the educational establishment is desperately seeking a national standard with a foolproof assessment process, many artists, museums, teachers and schools continue to resist a one-size-fits-all approach. Artists, like teachers, are wary of molds and are concerned about what is lost when copies are valued over originals. Artists protest the lack of beauty in many ways. They reveal the ugly and highlight the lies and secrets in ways that may make us uncomfortable. They ask us to question our values. The artist Barbara Kruger writes on a cropped photograph of a woman, "Do I have to give up me to be loved by you?" Without her words, the picture sends out a very different message. Coupling word and image helps us to raise questions about both.

It is curious that the acceptance or collapse of a particular art form or curriculum depends less on its content than on the powers that support it. The core curriculum at the University of Chicago has fewer challenges than the core at Brooklyn College. The Whitney Museum of Art can probably gaze into the future with greater abandon than a small, midwestern museum that is exhibiting postmodern art. A mayor and a governor are better positioned to determine school curricula than a group of teachers.

When seventeenth-century relics of human remains reside in prestigious religious and private collections, they are infinitely more acceptable and less shocking than the displays of body parts at a local tribal arts gallery. Joe Kincheloe suggests that celebrating the simplicity, spontaneity, and emotional power of non-Western art but simultaneously showing it in less prestigious places and labeling it "primitive" gives the public a duplicitous coded message. Paintings done in the Middle Ages of butchered animals find their hermeneutical home in the Louvre, but an animal rights painting by Sue Coe showing an equally gruesome scene of angry animal ghosts with the words, "Go Vegetarian" cannot find its place in a museum. The works of Hieronymus Bosch, a Dutch painter of the fifteenth century, whose terrifying and devilish realistic paintings of life on earth and in hell are hung in major European museums. In our times, a different hell may be depicted showing horrific truths about the inequities of gender, race, class, and ethnicity. These works may call forth the decency committees and are consigned to alternate spaces or permanently hidden from view. It took over twenty years and storage in a variety of warehouses for Judy Chicago's monumental and disturbing feminist work, "The Dinner Party" to find a permanent display space at The Brooklyn Museum of Art. Further issues arise when art goes public and shows up on the sides of buses, on television, on newsstands or in classrooms. When it is not in a museum, it is sometimes labeled "outsider" art. Location! Location! Location! Who decides and why?

Passionate Participation

Postmodern artists are shaking up traditions about the purposes of art when they direct our attention to previously "unnoticed" features. At the Corcoran Gallery in Washington, D.C., Ken Aptekar (1997) reinterpreted historical paintings in tandem with viewers and forges new and mysterious connections. He invited children, museum guards, fine arts students and other visitors to the museum to engage in a series of discussions from which Aptekar develops narrative texts. This is accomplished by creatively re-painting masterworks and sandblasting these new texts on glass panels. This interactive activity among the artist and the spectators heightens awareness of the depth and breadth of meaning that can be gleaned when we invite people to reflect about the relationship between art and object, art and personal interaction. The invitation to think for oneself and to re-interpret and even interrupt the canonical conversation is flourishing.

Viewers at the Williams College Museum of Art are asked to intervene in a series of exhibits entitled "Labeltalk" (1999-2001). For these exhibits, the museum selected very different objects from varying periods and asked Williams College professors to write a short response from the point of view of their discipline or scholarly interest. A historian looks at an eighteenth-century Hogarth painting of strolling actresses very differently from a professor of theater. A professor of political science viewing the famous Philippe Halsman photograph of Marilyn Monroe writes about the connection between violence and glamour. A female philosophy professor states that despite her victimhood, she hopes that Marilyn is encouraging women to transgress the usual stereotypes of female beauty. The visitors to the museum also write their responses.

This approach suggests pedagogical guidelines for teachers. Just as the professors were invited to consider the various interpretations that may extend the singular voice of a museum label, so too can teachers and students in an interdisciplinary spirit be empowered to engage uniquely with a work of art or an accepted educational practice. Good teaching should invite furious, passionate conversations. For meaning does not lie static within the object, the curriculum or the discourse. It bursts like a hatching bird from the ensuing dialogue. When the visitors to the Corcoran Gallery, the professors from Williams College and students in our classes enter into the conversation, their collaboration creates new knowledge as well as a community that has taken upon itself the responsibility for knowing.

Aestheticizing Teaching

Joe Kincheloe writes about the artist, Juan Gris, whose collages used common materials such as crayons, pasted paper, coffee cups and spoons to aestheticize the artifacts of the everyday world. This kind of transformation and re-presentation of the world can be replicated by creative, socially conscious teachers as they encourage students to look at the world in new ways. To live means to question reality and now hyperreality. At first, when Betty Friedan decided to get up from the kitchen floor, and Andy Warhol asked us new questions about Brillo boxes and Audre Lorde queried "Ain't I a Woman Too?" they may have enraged us. But then they changed us. Aesthetic experiences resist the anesthesia caused by the epidural of mindless submission. "Who's afraid of Virginia Woolf?" queried Edward Albee. . .the answer seems to be "nothing to fear as long as we're talking." Artful encounters may be painful, but they can also be wake-up calls that give us new eyes.

A commodified, technological society which values speed over self-consciousness requires that we re-think how we teach. Encounters with art promote an interior dialogue and today's teachers and children desperately need the arts so that they can be alone with their thoughts. In the *Age of Distraction*, Joseph R. Urgo (2000) points to the importance of the interior realm and the need to deny oneself constant access to the technologies by exerting control over what is ingested intellectually. How though, do we ask students in this technological age to forfeit the seduction of the quick fix? The answer may lie in the heady recognition of one's own personal agency which is encouraged by engagement with the arts. An electronic age makes greater demands on teachers to be artful. How else could a human "in your face" teacher teach? Most of us are not darting about, jumping on tables, altering our costumes and twitching like a television screen. Our frame doesn't change every seven seconds, and some students are alienated by the slow pace.

However, in defense of students, too often schools are grim places where joylessness presides. Most students show up every day but, in effect, are absent throughout their many years of schooling. Bombarded with a hyperreality whose speed and power leave little time to raise questions or personally mediate their world, many students can't even imagine a different life. They ask far too few questions of themselves, their teachers and their own epistemological baggage. A few are saved by teachers who return to students the ability to dream by making a connection between heart and mind. A classroom where art is an environmental surround helps teachers and students know that feelings matter and that emotions transmitted through expressive forms provide knowledge. Art experiences can open a window on a more comfortable world, one with less twitching and fewer distractions.

Arts, Literacy and Lincoln Center Institute

This book views the preparation of teachers through the lens of aesthetic education. In 1994, the Lincoln Center Institute in Manhattan and Brooklyn College entered into a partnership designed to heighten the aesthetic awareness of undergraduates and their instructors. An unusually talented group of teaching artists in collaboration with faculty from Brooklyn College, buttressed by live performances and museum visits, crossed literal and figurative bridges between the boroughs of Brooklyn and Manhattan, the arts and teaching. For some students, crossing the bridge, was a giant step, literally and metaphorically. Ramona King showed us how our bodies might communicate even better than our words. Diane Ramo taught us to dance our names. Tom Cabanis empowered us to sing scat and be-bop, and John Toth helped us to discover Mondrian in our own line drawings. David Gonzales transformed Orpheus forever into a guitar-playing hippie and helped teaching artists and professors to conflate teacher education and the aesthetic way of knowing. Most importantly, professors and teaching artists entered each other's communities blending the usual boundaries of their work.

My particular agenda has been to highlight the connections between literacy and the arts, mindful not to diminish the integrity of the work of art itself. The rigor and limitations of each art form can assist teachers to develop the language to express how the arts provide tangible and useful segues for teaching literacy. What follows are some suggestions in the language of the schools that attend to literacy concepts.

Schema theory, the expectations that we bring to the text, sometimes called cognitive mapping, assists the reader to bring forth what he or she already knows about the text and context. The arts activate prior knowledge. When Tom Cabanis connected teachers to the "Trout Quintet," he sought a point of entry that called upon their prior knowledge. By exploring their previous experiences with abstractions, their familiarity with the sounds in the piece and their awareness and ability to imitate sounds of deep emotion, he was able to build new levels of meaning going from the known to the unknown.

Similarly, teachers who are building the literacy skills of children carefully attend to their prior knowledge and open zones of proximal development. For example, when developing readiness for reading, we may show children Henri Rousseau's painting "The Sleeping Gypsy" to prompt storytelling. This famous painting, widely available in postcard reproductions, depicts a lion standing near a sleeping woman who has a stringed instrument at her side. The setting appears to be a desert. The context, as well as the figure/ground configuration is pivotal. Asking children to recall personal experiences and fantasies about lions, relationships between people and animals and then to tell a story prepares the child to appreciate the significance of sequence, detail, character and mood. This essential reading skill is developed as we assist children to organize experiences narratively. The segue is constructed by connecting the work of art to the child's experiences.

Other literacy skills and tasks that can be developed through aesthetic experiences are described in later chapters. These include:

1. Connecting visual and verbal responses
2. Developing thought using symbol systems that do not rely solely on oral and written responses
3. Attending to detail, sequence, context and inferences
4. Organizing experiences narratively
5. Developing critical skills of analysis through awareness of angle of vision
6. Interpreting and evaluating
7. Recognizing multiple and related ways of representing experience

Thought About Feeling

It is always a struggle to understand how thought about feeling is expressed in different forms, but repeated exposures to this way of working will center rather than dislocate. As teachers think about the relationship between the aesthetic and the intellectual, they develop pedagogical strategies that encourage engagement. It is a collaborative endeavor to aestheticize the familiar and to intellectualize the aesthetic. This involves the recognition of multiple ways of knowing which assists more students to discover that they are imaginative, creative and smart. The identification of those moments when we honor our expressiveness, see with new eyes or hear with keener ears prepares us to walk on both sides of the street in our personal and professional lives. Preservice teachers need to engage with works of art in safe spaces. They need to explore the relationship between works of art and the self as a rehearsal for their future crossings with students when they will reconstruct information into artful curricula.

Traditionally in education, the arts have been the province of specialists. Classroom teachers "did" art after the intellectual activities of the day, often unaware of the rigorous cognitive understandings that emerge from aesthetic engagement with the interior lives of students. Today, many educators know how to mine the arts to build skills and understandings without denying the integrity of the work of art. The arts stimulate thinking, forge connections and answer many of our teaching questions. Because experiences in the arts invite us to create, imagine and connect to something that we care for, they encourage our attention. When we ask students to sing songs of freedom, write about outsiderness, develop a rap from a poem, construct dioramas about the Depression or dress up in the clothing of their heritage, we honor and link their private and public selves. Life and life in classrooms become intertwined and school seems real.

However, in many schools, art is a frill, misunderstood and slotted into Friday afternoons when nothing very important happens anyway. Sometimes descriptions of what it means to engage with the arts is loaded down with the baggage of obscure language which exclude a potential receiver's participation. Those who have a vested interest in making the art experience an exclusive club perpetuate this mystification. Like much of schooling, the recognized "authorities" carry considerable weight. The extant epistemological frame is deeply rooted.

Modernist art movements such as expressionism and cubism pushed against the boundaries of their predecessors and postmodernism re-positioned itself against modernist perspectives ushering in another era. However, a new elitism with vested interests still pervades the art world and excludes the masses from the secret codes of their clubs. The public is infantilized and treated like the child who is sent to the principal's office. Reflection and critical thinking about works of art are frequently commandeered by a changing elite and overnight books are censored, museums threatened with closing and all varieties of art labeled like poisonous vials with dire warnings about the physical side effects brought about by exposure.

There is a strange inconsistency about art matters. From some quarters, it is viewed as subversive and considered a major contributor to declining moral standards. But for others, the advent of new technologies combined with deep concerns about the ugly underbelly of society, has spawned a new and daring kind of art focused on inequities. The notion that art can matter for different reasons to people from varying cultures, persuasions, occupations and eras has been resisted throughout the centuries. As Philip Yenawine notes, "The view of art as elitist and nonessential continues to cloud political commentary on the subject to this day" (1999, p. 11). Therefore, when teacher educators pre-empt art experiences for purposes of improving the insights, pedagogy and curricula of the schools, they meet enormous resistance. Despite the eloquent evidence that art experiences inform, clarify, transform and unite intellectual and imaginative processes, they are viewed with suspicion. In suggesting that art has a significant function in opening up new pathways for knowing is not to exclude the long and valid history of viewing art for its own sake. It is both possible and practical to maintain the integrity of the art itself while simultaneously appreciating its potential for understanding larger themes, building cognition and developing empathic competence. We ask in future chapters: What is art for? What does art do for people? Why do people create art? How can aesthetic experiences enhance learning?

This book highlights the ways in which teachers and students through multifaceted encounters with art and culture have begun to rethink and redesign the educational process. Multicultural classrooms require that teachers act as change agents, bridging the chasm between themselves, their students, and the culture. The art experience with its potential to quicken thought about feeling can provide a wellspring of knowledge about curriculum and pedagogy. From preschool through the doctoral seminar, it should not be a question of developing universal aesthetic tastes but the more fruitful effort of identifying and articulating the connections among aesthetic feeling, empathic competence and intellectual understanding.

References

Aptekar, Ken (1997). *Talking to picture*. Catalogue of an Exhibition at the Corcoran Gallery of Art, Washington, D.C.

Urgo, Joseph R. (2000). *Age of distraction*. Jackson: University Press of Mississippi.

Williams College Museum of Art (1999-2001). *Labeltalk*. Williamstown, MA.

Yenawine, P. (1999). But what has changed? In B. Wallis, Marianne Weems & P. Yenawine (Eds.). *Art matters: how the culture wars changed America*. New York: New York University Press.

Three

Says Who? Who Decides What Is Art?

Joe L. Kincheloe

In this chapter I want to view art in context, to ask some questions about art and its social, political and educational roles. In this process I want to put forward some thoughts about elitism, marginalization and the forces that help construct art's relationship to a variety of domains. The following list of questions drives this chapter:

- Who decides what is art/artifact?
- When does an artifact become art?
- Does the location (place) of the art/artifact determine whether it is art?
- What is the relationship between art/artifact and the culture that produces it? Evaluates it?
- What does power have to do with art/artifact?
- What benefits do we derive from encounters with art/artifact? What liabilities?
- Is there "good art" and "bad art"?
- Should art be judged on a scale of quality? Whose scale?
- What is included in the notion of aesthetic?
- Do aesthetic experiences involve the pursuit of beauty? Should they?
- Is beauty always good?
- What are the political consequences of art and art criticism?
- Do function, form and technique/skill play a role in the study of art/artifact?
- Must art include function, form and technique/skill to be art?

- Is meaning always intended in the production of art/artifact? Who makes the meaning?
- Does art/artifact always exist in a context?

When analysts study the ways individuals in different periods of time and different cultural settings make decisions about what constitutes good art, they uncover a variety of issues that help them understand not only art but the culture that produced it. This concept grounds my interest in art and art criticism—I admit it I'm first and foremost a culturalist who is interested in making sense of who we are as humans, how we got this way and where we are going (or should go). Thus, my interest in art criticism is not simply to learn about art—though art is extremely important. I study art and art criticism to learn about culture, cognition (creativity), human possibility and history. From my perspective understanding art is not just a frill, an adornment that sets those who have it apart from those who don't. Such knowledge is a central part of a rigorous education that makes us smarter, more insightful, more sensitive to what is occurring around us—in other words better educated people who are more capable of working toward democratic, egalitarian social change.

As a culturalist I see human beings as meaning makers who inscribe meaning in everything they do. These meanings are not absolute but contingent on an exceedingly complex network of other socially and historically contextualized meanings and interpretations. Many of these cultural understandings become so commonplace in particular societies that they come to be viewed as indisputable truths, "common sense." Thus, culturalists view art as one of many types of cultural texts to be "read" for the various meanings made around it. In the process we learn about art producers, their audiences and, importantly, ourselves. Here we begin to see how we are part of a social and historical context that produces meaning in ways we never before appreciated. Examining a piece of art we find that our culture has trained/educated us to view it, unwittingly, in particular ways. In this manner we bring to the surface for examination culturally constructed aspects of ourselves and the people around us. This introspective process is a central part of what many consider a democratic education—gaining an awareness of who we are and how we came to be that way.

Thus, a basic question arises here concerning how we judge painting and sculpture, as well as other artistic cultural productions including literature, music, dance, architecture and cultural criticism itself. Is artistic value determined by an artwork's essence or by its context? This is not simply a key question of art criticism but the way we answer it shapes the way we structure education, the nature of our social and political perspectives and the types of people we might want to become. Because of its importance, we will return to the question frequently. At this point it is becoming obvious that we study art not simply for art's sake but as part of a larger attempt to make sense of the world, ourselves and our relation to the world. From my perspective such study is a part of a larger attempt to be rigorously educated, to become something more than we presently are. It induces us to consider from a different direction what the world is and ought to be. It induces us to think of our personal role in this life-affirming process, to examine the difference between ethical and unethical actions.

Culture Wars: The Struggle Over Artistic/Social Meaning

Questions of aesthetic/artistic value must be constantly negotiated. And negotiated they are daily and often vociferously at the beginning of the twenty-first century. So contentious have these contemporary debates become that many analysts contend that we are living in an era of culture wars. The war is observed in public controversies over school curricula, movie ratings, TV programming, public funding for the arts, museum exhibitions, the look of skyscapes in urban areas, etc. . . . Aesthetic values are no longer secure, as individuals from all over the world join in the debate over what constitutes great art, beauty, vulgarity, or compelling originality. To be aware of the forces shaping the early twenty-first century it is important to be knowledgeable of this debate. It is the contention of many culturalists that the elite guardians of the art world have been unreflective about the traditional ways artistic value is determined. Unchallenged cultural assumptions often permeate such determinations and the interests they serve remain unexposed.

Culturalists maintain that it is in the best interests of society to shake up the guardians of tradition with basic questions concerning art, criticism and social values. It is their role, they argue, to point out previously unnoticed features of a work in a way that offers a profound insight into the nature of the artist, his or her audience, critics and the culture in which all of these agents operate. In this pursuit culturalists make use of literature/literary criticism, political analysis, sociology, anthropology, philosophy and history to view art and through art, society in creative new frames. Interestingly the practice of art is being reconfigured in exciting new ways. Connecting social theory—defined as an act of attempting to make sense of and maybe change for the better the social world around us—to the artistic enterprise exposes assumptions about the ways knowledge and meaning are produced. The consciousness such understandings engender allows artists in different domains to go beyond existing boundaries as the artificial divisions between art and education, art and politics and art and cultural analysis are removed. When such boundaries are transgressed the possibilities for previously uncharted artistic work increase dramatically. Art crosses not only disciplinary boundaries but moves across other demarcation lines as well, connecting text to audience and art to everyday life (Stossel, 1998; Wilson, 1993; Ruesga, 1996; Best and Kellner, 1991).

However, in the cultural war over artistic/social meaning many contend that the preceding pronouncements muddle the debate over the evaluation of good and bad art. If artistic values have to be constantly negotiated, then traditional questions such as "are there consistencies in what constitutes good art?" or "are there clear distinctions between so-called high art and low art?" need to be asked and discussed in an exploratory manner. I use the term *exploratory* in the sense that such discussions should attempt to identify the assumptions and values that shape differing positions. These interchanges need to take place, if for no other reason, to point out how little agreement exists concerning the basis on which aesthetic judgments are tendered. The search for a method to validate claims of artistic value has yielded scant results. Of course, the search becomes more difficult as culturalists delineate the existence of many different systems of evaluation. On what basis do we choose between such systems? "Uniformity amidst variety? Formal unity? Expressiveness?" (Ruesga, 1996). No one knows exactly what even these phrases might mean.

Thus, embedded in every act of art criticism is a social theory, held either tacitly or consciously. Stated differently, the way we make sense of the world shapes our aesthetic evaluations whether we are aware of it or not. In addition to the tacit or explicit social theoretical connection to criticism, those who judge artistic quality seem to concern themselves with the work's relationship to the historical period and cultural location of its production. Such factors are often claimed to be peripheral to "pure aesthetic" judgments, but analysis indicates that despite protestations to the contrary they exert a profound influence. Indeed, in more classical forms of criticism the idea that art is shaped by social theoretical assumptions and tacit views of the world constitutes a bastardization of the purity of the aesthetic process (Wilson, 1993; Turner, 1996).

Questions of art vis-à-vis power seem to make more traditional critics queasy, as "cultural barbarians" ask: Who says this is great art? Who has the right to designate this piece a part of the official canon of artistic greatness? Would the aesthetic gatekeepers include those critics who write for high art journals or hang around hip galleries in the village? Who draws the line between the high and the low? Between good and bad tastes? What role do highbrow critics bequeath to power and other sociological forces? What happens when these powerful critics disagree—as they inevitably do? Thus, we return to our notion that these issues of judgment have to be brought to the public consciousness, they have to be constantly negotiated. What is low art today may be considered high art tomorrow—Shakespeare's plays, for example, were very popular as a low art form in his day but were not considered a manifestation of canonical high art for years after his death. Thus, the high art designation is never static, as it shifts with the times (Cowen, 1999; Ruesga, 1996).

The Arbiters of Aesthetic Quality: The Trouble with High Art

Allow me to expose my biases up front: I am not comfortable with modernist means of determining the worth of art. When I hear many experts delineate the impenetrable boundary between good art and bad art, I sweat. Please understand this propensity as you read my chapters and judge my words. My concern in this chapter revolves around the social, cultural, cognitive, political and educational meanings of these artistic/aesthetic dynamics, how we might better understand them, and how we might become smarter about art and aesthetics in particular and about ourselves and the world around us in general. I do not accept the myth perpetuated in Western societies that what is called "high art" or the "classics" is profoundly different and superior to other types of cultural productions. Exposure to these "grand artifacts" of high culture will not automatically make us "cultured" (I think this implies that one who is cultured is of more worth than one who is not) and intelligent. Such an elitist view seems to assume that these artifacts possess a magical power to instill an elite status on those who hang around them.

Having rejected the magic of high art, I am not making the argument that we ignore it, burn it, or ban it from the educational curriculum. Such artifacts, the process by which they were granted high status and the values implicit within this process are important subjects in any contemporary education. My point here is to question these artifacts and the process of the sanctification, not to hold them up for distant admiration from the cultural barbarians and their untrained eyes. Such a process of demystification, I believe, serves the best interests of a democratic society, as we begin to understand that the differences between the "high" and "low" are not as great as we might have imagined. Indeed, we may find that "objective" judgments of quality may have less to do with particular aesthetic concerns than with cultural values, class dynamics, ideologies and even ethnic, racial and gender issues. Such understandings may not simply change our perspectives toward art and aesthetics but may transform the way we see ourselves and the world. This is, of course, one of many reasons that I find these issues so important to all of us in the twenty-first century (Allen, 1995).

Indeed, in the first decade of the twenty-first century there is renewed effort on the part of the guardians of cultural standards to separate the highest artistic and aesthetic expression from popular or mass art. High art, such cultural trolls at the bridge tell us, is universal and for all times; low or popular art appeal only to particular times and places and exploit those of us who consume them by posing as if they understand our particular circumstances. Thus, they appeal, it is argued, to our baser instincts, in this case to our narcissism (Ruesga, 1996).

Such pronouncements are particular aspects of the elite practice of paradigm enforcement. Such regulation is the *raison d'être* of particular institutions that validate or censure particular artist works or workers. The official condemnation of the Brooklyn Museum's Sensation exhibit could be considered an example of this paradigm enforcement. As a form of low art, Sensation was deemed a "deviant production" by particular cultural brokers. An elitism infuses these boundary drawers as they set themselves apart from the unwashed. The uneducated in this context are not deemed to have the ability to comprehend the sophistication of the elite's aesthetic concerns. As the aesthetic guardians validate and censure, they attempt to remove art from the distasteful realm of the ideological so that connoisseurs can focus on the formal aspects (e.g., form, technique and style) of art. The concept of "art for art's sake" becomes the driving concern of the elite formalists.

In every form of artistic expression formalist modernist constructs of art attempted to attend only to those specific features of the form—e.g., what elements are specific to music, painting, writing, sculpting, etc. . . . Modernism emerged in the early nineteenth century delineating new artistic perspectives that reflected the larger social and intellectual changes of the Age of Reason and its concurrent scientific revolution.

Operating in a methodical and often scientific manner modernist artists sought to keep differing artistic forms separate and pursue the formal aspects of each form. Over the last two centuries various groups would question these assumptions. By the 1960s postmodernists would call into question a long line of modernist and "high art" assumptions. In our exploration of art and the cultures that produce it and assess it this postmodern rebellion against modernist art helps us conceptualize and develop our questions about artistic endeavor and its cultural meanings. We will return to these postmodern themes in this chapter.

As postmodernists questioned the sacred tenets of modernist form and technique, such inquiries were viewed as signs of aesthetic decline and even anti-intellectualism. Postmodern artists were offended by modernism's artificial boundaries between diverse art forms, between artistic creation and audience, between art and life, between high and low art, between elite and mass culture and between art producer and consumer. Such perspectives induced postmodernists to pose questions about the entire enterprise of art that elicit new insights into "the way the art world works." My concerns in this chapter are influenced by such postmodernist apprehensions and will be recognized throughout my portions of this book. In this context I advocate a democratic aesthetic that refuses to surrender artistic judgment to an elite pantheon of arbiters of taste. Just as I advocate in other contexts that teachers, workers and other citizens take charge of the production of knowledge in their particular domains, I contend here that artistic production and aesthetic evaluation become the province of everyone. In such a democratic context we may find that the arts become a part of more and more people's everyday lives and less an esoteric realm unfriendly to everyday people (Brown, 1995; Best and Kellner, 1991).

Very simple and commonsensical questions about the world of art—such as who gave him the right to determine artistic worth?—seem to sometimes send the guardians of culture into fits of rage. Confronted with such intelligent questions they often retreat to the safety of proclamations of cultural decline, "You wouldn't ask such a question if we weren't suffering from a *loss of standards*," they proclaim. In the world of the aesthetic elite it seems that the mere raising of analytical questions about artistic quality and the basis on which they are made, is an assault on the sanctity of Western civilization and the grace of America. It was such questioning, many argue, that brought about the "American fall from grace" in the 1960s. This alleged fall from grace was marked by a decline in aesthetic, artistic and educational standards, a moral crisis and a deterioration of

American eminence. The inseparability of the aesthetic issues raised here from social, cultural and political dimensions seems apparent, as the guardians deem the decline in one domain to be inseparable from decline in another.

In the case of the 1960s and the popular art it produced the guardians of aesthetic and corresponding standards have maintained for four decades that such "art" and the successors it inspired have undermined Western and American cultural stability and the traditional standards of quality on which the society was grounded. In the minds of the guardians such productions were not only "low/bad art" but possessed the social power to shake the very foundations of society (Percy, 1999). As Karel Rose writes in this volume, the guardians often move to suppress that which does not meet their aesthetic standards, often as in the case in question by issuing "dire warnings about the physical side effects brought about by exposure." In this suppressive role the guardians' actions display fascistic tendencies. The vehemence, for example, with which New York Mayor Rudolph Giuliani reacted to the 1999 Sensation exhibit seems oddly out of proportion to the socio-aesthetic dynamics of the display. Throughout Giuliani's attacks on the exhibit one can discern the assumption that art such as Sensation has the power to undermine American society—such art is an aesthetic terrorist bomb. At the very least Sensation and "bad art" like it are to be feared and suppressed in the aesthetic judgments of many of the guardians.

Such paradigm enforcements are reminiscent of the actions of Egyptian guardians of aesthetic standards in the third millennium B.C. To protect their society from the negative effects of "bad art," aesthetic authorities mandated what colors, designs and artistic forms artists could use in their work. Dictates become so detailed that human representation had to meet exacting rules: "the ankle on the first horizontal level, knee on the sixth level, shoulder on the sixteenth level" (Brown, 1995, p. 140). Implicit in Mayor Giuliani's pronouncements on Sensation was the dictate that cow dung cannot be used in public art. Aesthetic fear and aesthetic enforcement have a long history. Returning to Karel Rose's point about the protective activities of the guardians, reconsider her assertion that "the public is infantilized, treated like the child sent to the principal's office and often not allowed to decide what is 'good' or 'bad,' 'high' or 'low.'" Such aesthetic policy, of course, could not take place if the guardians did not believe that the public is incapable of understanding "great art." We alone, the guardians conclude, are capable of making aesthetic judgments (Cowen, 1999).

The socio-aesthetic position of the guardians of high art is more than merely a conservative view of culture. Guardians, I contend in this chapter, come from all political and cultural positions. Embedded within many of the guardians' thinking is an unwavering belief in an artistic and even cultural canon that transcends time and place. In this rarefied canonical realm meanings of "the great art of Western culture" are not up for discussion and do not change when viewed from different cultural or paradigmatic locations or in differing historical eras. In short, they are fixed, timeless and transhistorical. With the canon secured and, importantly, *beyond questioning*, profound social, political and educational implications emerge from the exalted world of high art. While I am not seeking the status of some stylized iconoclasm, I cannot help but argue that the aesthetic orthodoxy of the guardians of high culture does not operate to provide higher-order insight into the realm of artistic evaluation or sociocultural concerns.

Indeed, in a context shaped by this type of sacred canonical management of art and aesthetics all a teacher can *legitimately* do is present a body of inert, intractable information about high art, its unnegotiable meaning and the specific features that make it great. Students are rendered passive receivers of such data and are positioned in an infantilized role. Indeed, I do not deem it improper to argue that in such canonical approaches to art, those who are indoctrinated by the guardians of aesthetic truth are stupidified to the degree they fail to question the process. This "questioning of the process" so infuriating to the guardians of high art is key to the rigorous scholarly process advocated here in a democratic art education. In the name of an elite, high quality education great art is taught in a cognitive, social and educational context that is reductionistic in its decontextualization, historical amnesia and dismissal of the complexity of the dynamics that shape artistic production and reception. Not only is pedagogy reduced and critical thinking undermined, but even deliberations over aesthetic value and artistic significance themselves are intellectually diluted in this "exalted" context.

Just who are the barbarians in this context? Who are the aesthetically impoverished? While I am by no means willing to ascribe these descriptions to anyone in the domain of art or aesthetics, I hope these elitists who have traditionally used such terms will reconsider their practices. In this context it is important to note that such damnable elitism is not the province of some bygone era where tuxedo-clad muck-a-mucks sipped fine champagne at Jay Gatsby's estate and made snide comments about the limitations of the "common stew." It is alive and well in many elevated quarters in the contemporary era. It can be found in many domains and movements of all stripes, including a few of the "return to beauty" advocates of the last decade who seek a "pure aesthetic" free from the muddling influence of social theory and cultural analysis. Such modes of investigation bring entirely too many elements of the rabble into the genteel world of the fine arts and the restricted exalted status it so sweetly provides (Allen, 1995; Stossel, 1998).

Rebellions in Modernism: Complexities and Contradictions

My interest in an anti-elitist, socially and culturally contextualized, humbly iconoclastic, politically transformative study of art draws me inexorably to the work of the avant-garde artists (the cubists, surrealists, dadaists and expressionists, for example) of the early twentieth century. The avant-garde satire of the pomposity of the institution of art and its separation from life inform the type of historically and culturally contextualized, cognitively enhancing, socially transformative and politically engaged form of art study and art education promoted in this chapter. At the same time, however, the modernist avant-garde's social and political contradictions and the cultural problems emerging from them are also instructive to those concerned with social change and social justice. The complex relationship between their brilliant works of conceptual and visual art and the cultural blindnesses of their time make the cubists, surrealists, dadaists and abstract expressionists fascinating grist for our analytical mill.

From the first time I encountered the artists of the modernist avant-garde—not in school in my case but in my independent studies in early adulthood—I was entranced with the brilliance of their ideas. The artistic and conceptual insights provided by Rene Magritte, Juan Gris, Georges Braque and their cubist colleagues induced me to think of new ways of seeing the world. I was particularly struck by their notion of multiple perspectives of an object. If an artist or a cultural analyst looks at the world only from a familiar perspective, he or she is providing only a fragment of the information needed to gain a compelling insight into an object and its relationship to other objects. To an ambitious but unexposed kid from the mountains of Tennessee this insight provided a unique angle in the effort to gain a divergent view of the cosmos. It provided motivation to seek new and different ways of seeing familiar entities.

I was also entranced by the avant-garde's disdain of the formal quest to produce beautiful art. In alienated times the mere pursuit of beauty and form seemed trivial, they argued. Picasso himself maintained that artistic education in beauty is fraudulent and, other avant-gardists contended, part of our charge is to break down the mandated cultural divisions separating "the beautiful" from "the ugly." In the same oppositional mode avant-garde art, cubism in particular, challenged Western Cartesian-Newtonian notions of time as a linear stream consistently flowing from past to future. At the same time the cubists challenged particular Western ways of seeing, they still were rational modernists as they sought to produce art that contained purer forms, shapes and lines that would lead artists to better represent "the truth" in their paintings (Best and Kellner, 1991; Padgham, 1988).

As seekers of purity in form and truth, many artists in the various movements of the avant-garde sought the heroic possibilities of modernism. Inscribed in this heroism was a belief in progress and individualism and the superiority of Western culture. The point worth making here is, of course, the complexity of modernist avant-gardism. Embedded within the work of the cubists, surrealists, dadaists and expressionists are contradictory heroic, male-centered, rationalistic and white supremacist impulses existing side-by-side with a discomfort with Western material values, the culture's emotional repression, its monoculturalism and its provincialism. Any effort to discuss the cultural dynamics, the cognitive insights and the educational/curricular value of the avant-garde must constantly take into account these paradoxes. One of the features of this revealing avant-garde tendency for contradiction that will be examined throughout the rest of this chapter involves the artists' use of content and forms from nonwhite cultures, or as many of the artists expressed it—"primitivism" (Jordan and Weedon, 1995).

Learning the Multiple Lessons of the Modernist Avant-Garde: Negotiating the Complexities and Contradictions

In many ways the modernist avant-garde becomes a case study for the relationship among art, culture, cognition, politics and education: We learn both from the avant-gardists' brilliance and naiveté and the complexity of the relationship between the two dynamics. While in cubism we gain subtle insight into the way the world and human perceptions of it operate by simultaneous multiple perceptions of an object from numerous angles, we also understand that cubist artists believe that such multi-perspectives provided the "true reality" of an object. Embedded in such a belief is a modernist assumption that through reason we can provide a final truth about the nature of the cosmos. In light of social theoretical advances of the last few decades, such an assumption seems quite naive.

Despite this naiveté—that I so arrogantly assert with the benefit of 20-20 hindsight—cubist artists anticipated the postmodern turn of the latter half of the twentieth century. A good example of such anticipation would involve Juan Gris's development of collage, his desire to aestheticize the artifacts of the everyday world and his playfulness with appearances that would influence so many artists of the late 1950s, 1960s, and beyond. Gris and many other modernist avant-gardists induced their postmodern progeny to erase the boundaries between art and life, undermine the autonomy of the artistic domain and to redefine the notion of aesthetics. Also included in this group were the New York-based abstract expressionists who shared many of the cubists' discomfort with the goal of producing beautiful art. Profoundly influencing the later postmodern revolution, abstract expressionists pushed away the everyday world of objects and started from scratch with new insights into color, shapes, lines and forms.

The string of expressionist movements consistently worked to distort comfortable modes of representation in painting, film, architecture and even literature and drama to express the emotions and private concerns of the artist. The personal feelings of the expressionists, their discomforts with Western social failures, were so intense that they found realistic depictions inadequate to the task of articulating them. In painting, such affective intensities were projected by distortions of traditional forms, shocking colors, weighty lines and the turbulent use of the paintbrush. Despite their passions and discomforts the expressionists were mostly bourgeoisie individuals with little interest in the political domain. Consistent with the contradictions of the modernist avant-garde, the expressionists were deeply offended by the oppression of bourgeoisie family life and its relationship to capitalism and industrialization. Nonetheless, they rarely involved themselves in political movements of any type.

Adamant in their refusal to "beautify" the world, expressionists such as Jackson Pollack, Franz Klilne, William de Kooning and Barnett Newman (notice a male dominance here?) paradoxically based their work on a rejection of the Western status quo while simultaneously shying away from overt political statements in their paintings. Sensing that realism in art strong-arms an oppressive and simplistic notion of truth while protecting the mind from uncertainty, the expressionists carried on the avant-garde resistance to fatuous representations of "reality." Jackson Pollack is the best known of the angry abstract expressionists, moving abstraction and nonrepresentation to new levels. Pollack came to represent the modernist notion of anti-hero—represented so well in cinema by the image of James Dean—with its desire for significations of the grand, the permanent, the towering, and the masculinity of originality. Such abstract expressionism would influence artists such as Robert Rauschenberg and Jasper Johns who would move such work into a postmodern domain.

Dadaism—which moved, amused, and inspired me—has been described more as an attitude than a style of art. Tristan Tzara, the author of Dada manifestos, captured the attitude with his proclamation: "We demand the right to piss in different colors" (Jordan and Weedon, 1995, p. 341). The origins of Dadaism provide profound insight into the ways art, culture, politics, and cognition come together in world-changing ways throughout historical and cultural time zones. Emerging as an orphan of World War I who had witnessed millions of young men dying or hoping to die in soon forgotten trenches, Dadaism burst forth in Zurich of the 1920s. Attempting to shock a complacent middle-class world out of its sociopolitical sleep, young artists produced disorienting works that reveled in their bad taste. Marcel Duchamp, for example, presented a urinal as a piece of art in an attempt to shock the art world out of its comfortable assumptions about the art, aesthetics, culture, and the political realm. The urinal, since its exhibition, has become a symbol of dadaist subversion of established art.

Another modernist avant-garde movement, surrealism, attempted to produce art and artistic concepts that operated outside the influence of reason or a concern with aesthetics. Once this break was made, the surrealists maintained, artistic endeavor could recover all that was lost in modernist scientific attempts to repress the nonrational dimensions of the human mind. Such nonrational dimensions included the erotic, exotic, and the unconscious, and in this context surrealists worked to carefully connect art with philosophy and ways of seeing and transforming the social and political world. Surrealist theorist Andre Breton urged his audience to draw upon the power of their dream lives, the creative abilities of the unconscious, and the benefits of the myths of various cultures that unite us and move us to deeper levels of understanding. I am still inspired and seduced by the libidinal energy of the surrealists and the cultural and aesthetic critique they produced, the social and artistic possibilities they imagined (Padgham, 1988; Best and Kellner, 1991; Brown, 1995; Jordan and Weedon, 1995).

The Slippery Slopes of Modern Art: Avant-Garde Colonialism

No matter how much cubism, expressionism, Dadaism and surrealism might arouse us, it is necessary to note the contradictions within the movements and their failure to undermine oppressive ways of seeing and ideological constructs. One of the most important contradictions and dramatic failures of the modernist avant-garde—and a central concern of this chapter—involves the notion that much of the innovative power of the various avant-garde movements was appropriated from colonized and typically nonwhite peoples. Such appropriations were rarely acknowledged in a direct manner and when they were signaled the problematic term, primitivism was employed. In this failure to understand the relationship between themselves and the "primitive" other, the avant-garde artists provide us with negative lessons that I hope we have the wisdom to learn and apply to the art, cultural analysis, politics and education of our time. Unfortunately, as illustrated by the Sensation and other exhibits I'm afraid we still have far to go in the twenty-first century.

The racial politics of the modernist avant-garde placed the artists on a slippery cultural slope. The dadaists, for example, would be appalled to hear that their racial perspectives would be viewed as inscribed by racist tendencies by their successors—but, to me, there seems little doubt that racist dynamics permeated their artistic viewpoints. This point must be made very carefully and precisely. I do not believe that individual dadaist artists harbored racist disdain of Africans, Asian, Latino, or indigenous peoples. But in what they thought was a celebration of the virtues of such peoples, the dadaists exalted what they saw as their spontaneity, emotional power, irrationality, use of the body and simplicity. To the dadaists these were traits from which all repressed bourgeoisie Westerners could learn. Maybe there are lessons to be learned here, but the point that haunts the dadaist celebration is that these are the very characteristics that Europeans have traditionally used to prove the inferior status of what they considered primitive peoples.

In this racist ideological frame "people of color are musical, artistic, physical and emotional—thus, incapable of the reasoning powers and the cultural achievements of us white people." This is not what the dadaists meant, but this is what many Westerners understood their art to convey.

Inadvertently, the dadaist and other avant-garde artists bolstered the racial stereotypes and binarisms that were used as justifications for colonialism and other forms of Western racial oppression. Thus, the seeds of their cultural and political failures were sown in an inability to refrain from "otherizing" the nonwhite in their fascination with their cultural achievements and artistic genius.

For example, in the avant-garde's depictions of women of color the male artists too often merely reflected common racist views of dominant Western culture. The familiar themes of physicality, emotion and passion reemerge, only in the case of the otherized female they are eroticized in a lascivious sexual manner. There is little difference in this avant-garde view of the black women and that of white slave owners of previous centuries. Thus, African, Asian, Latino and indigenous women suffered a double objectification as both woman and racial other. These failures would not surface for decades; they would be understood only after a variety of liberation movements challenged Western peoples with their representations and treatment of "the other." In the shorter term avant-garde art had more immediate problems to confront.

In both the Soviet Union and Nazi Germany in the 1930s modern avant-gardism came to be seen as a threat to the state. In these regimes such art was violently squashed and only "safe" and "socially responsible" artistic forms were allowed. Modern avant-garde art in the U.S. during this era was contained and pacified in a much less brutal manner via its canonization in museums and universities and its commodification in the art market. Ironically, the works of artists who so loathed the bourgeoisie became upper-middle class status trophies and used to decorate the consumer society. Indeed, marketing, advertising and commercial design employed its forms and techniques as basic principles of their professional knowledge. "What a long, strange trip it's been" was as appropriate for the avant-garde artists as it would be for the Grateful Dead and the counterculture of the 1960s (Jordon and Weedon, 1995; Best and Kellner, 1991).

Increasingly, in the eyes of many in the late 1950s and 1960s, modernist avant-garde art had lost its driving passion, its freshness, its oppositionality. Contrary to the objectives of its creative generators, modern art was increasingly unable to reintegrate art into the pulse of everyday life as it was increasingly sanitized by its creeping institutionalization. With its obsession with constant change and "the new," it was vulnerable to capitalist mechanizing and elitist collaboration. In this context avant-gardism devolved into more a change of images than a force for political transformation. In this accommodationist reconceptualization of artistic avant-gardism, cultural analysts must return to the relationship of the racial other.

These African, Asian, Oceanic and indigenous others could be celebrated and even courted as long as they refrained from asserting their personhood and claiming an active place in the shaping of the history, the present and future of "modern" art. Thus, modern avant-garde art never came to terms with the fact that it had been a principal heir to the spoils of Western imperial brutality. Without such conquests and the power relations they established, progressive Western artists could not have enjoyed the accolades and material benefits bestowed on them as a result of the deployment of non-Western art. But as we have learned from the field of whiteness studies over the last decade or so: such are the benefits of white privilege. It is imperative that anti-racist cultural, political and artistic activities in the twenty-first century act on these racial understandings. They must install warning signs on the slippery racial slopes of the artworld. Who says what is art and the official history of art? In avant-garde modernism it was the Western white boys.

The Postmodern Challenge

As a simple matter of clarification, it is important to explain the complex and ambiguous uses of the term *postmodern* before we proceed with our discussion of art, aesthetics, culture, politics, cognition and education. Postmodernism questions the modernist faith in technology, its doctrine of progress, its cult of reason, its belief in the stability of language and meaning and its ability to isolate aspects of the world in order to better study and understand them. As postmodern observers subject to analysis of modernist notions about the social and cultural spheres, they admit previously inadmissible evidence produced by those previously excluded. In this way they challenge hierarchical structures of knowledge, evaluation and power that promote "experts" over the "masses." In the world of art, postmodernists have sought to undermine colonialist and masculinist assumptions about art and aesthetics. In the process they work to include women's and non-European art and to use feminist and multicultural perspectives to challenge the artistic/aesthetic assumptions of the Western male art establishment (Calinescu, 1987; Hebdige, 1989; Kincheloe and Steinberg, 1997).

This postmodernism or postmodern critique is not one single perspective but can better be understood by examining two differing branches. The first, ludic postmodernism, or a playful postmodernism is an approach to social theory that is not centered on the exposure and transformation of oppressive cultural, social and political power structures. Ludic postmodernism typically addresses what it describes as the playfulness of the signifier and the nature of the space between what is said and what is received. In this context ludic postmodernism concerns itself with the deconstruction of Western constructions of reality. In the midst of analyzing the slipperiness of Western meanings, ludic postmodernism, concludes that meaning itself is fragmented and ultimately undecidable. I find much danger in this orientation, for whether it means to or not, such a position props up the status quo by rendering meaning making and change impossible.

I am much more comfortable with an affirmative and democratic form of postmodernism that connects the deconstruction and other analytical forms of ludic postmodernism to the critique of lived social and cultural structures in the context of history. In this articulation postmodernism can serve as a pragmatic intervention to forms of Eurocentric, patriarchal, class elitist and white supremacist forms of regulation. The linguistic, textual and semiotic concerns of ludicism, affirmative/democratic postmodernists maintain, have real-life political, social, economic and cultural consequences. Representations shape human consciousness; and human ways of seeing the world profoundly influence the nature of everyday life and social relations. Without connections to structural power and an understanding of human suffering, affirmative postmodernism fears that ludicism will fall into nihilism.

Many novice readers of postmodern themes become confused by the distinction between postmodernism as previously described and postmodernity. Postmodernism is a critique of modernism, postmodernity is a social condition. Of course, the postmodern critique (postmodernism) and the postmodern condition (postmodernity) are closely connected; yet the attempt to distinguish them confuses many observers. Further complicating the matter is the realization that postmodernity cannot be seen as a simply homogenous historical period. All cultural expression in the contemporary era is not postmodern—just as all art produced in the postmodern condition is not postmodern (Smart, 1992; Borgmann, 1992; Kincheloe and McLaren, 2000). Advocates of a postmodern frame of reference always run the risk of overstating the uniqueness and newness of the concept. While we cannot simply deny the existence of a postmodern condition, neither can we simply assume its widespread existence without rigorous questioning and analysis.

When it exists, postmodernity is characterized by a social vertigo that emerges from a so-called cultural hyperreality caused by a loss of touch with traditional notions of time, self, community and history. New structures transform cultural space and time generated by bombarding electronic images from local, national and international locations shake our personal sense of place. Electronic transmissions move us in and out of different geographical and cultural locales instantaneously, juxtaposing nonlinear images of the world with homey, folksy and comfortable personalities who reassure us in the midst of the chaos (Gergen, 1991; Smart, 1992). Our contact with this postmodern condition or hyperreality diminishes our ability to find meaning to engender a passion for commitment. If the world is so crazy that we cannot make sense, then what conceivably merits our commitment? One of the charges of an affirmative/democratic postmodernism, therefore, is to make meaning of and make meaning *for* the inhabitants of the postmodern condition.

So, in the artistic domain modernism and postmodernism are used in the discursive universe delineated here. Again, for purposes of clarity modernist art usually is said to begin in the late nineteenth century and run at least through the middle of the twentieth century with an emphasis on establishing a universal view of art and aesthetics. Modern art set standards for the proper production, appreciation and critique of creative work. Postmodern art is said to have emerged in the 1950s and 1960s as—depending on which expert you ask—either a new movement discretely breaking from modernism or as a new phase of modernism. Many analysts choose not to use the term *postmodernism* because of the contradictions and uncertainties that surround it. I use it here because it signals some important changes in ways of seeing and in cultural politics that no other term captures. One of the most important features of the movement involved its discomfort with the modernist delineation of universality. This concept, the postmodernists contended, was more of an ethnocentric manifestation of subjectivity underwritten by power than an expression of aesthetic objectivity.

Aesthetic Confusion: The Postmodern Challenge to the Single Story of High Art

Thus, postmodernist art criticism questioned what it discerned was an elite and arrogant proclamation of universal standards for art. In the postmodernist eye modernism was always fearful of a "leveling down" that would erode intractable standards of quality. Such pure notions of art were challenged by new technologies such as photography and cinema that helped produce a disdain for tradition, an erosion of the special aura of the artist. These new technologies created a huge quantity of popular artifacts for the mass media. Artists would have to find a location in this new cultural domain for their work—a social process that continues to expand and complicates the lives of artists in the twenty-first century. In light of the challenges of this new context to traditional notions of art and the social role of artists, no one has any idea of where art goes from here. Postmodern art reflects this confusion.

Indeed, the inability to address or make sense of this contemporary confusion is an important aspect of the most nihilistic features of the ludic variety of postmodernism. In this theoretical context there is little use for studying the relationship between art, culture, politics, cognition and education because no one can find the way out of the chaos of the present cultural disorientation. A more affirmative/democratic postmodernism attempts to make meaning in this situation. Arguing that while contemporary "hyperreality" with its exploding information production and saturation of visual imagery may be confusing, we can begin to make sense of contemporary culture by abandoning the modernist quest for "one story" to explain it. Such critical postmodernists argue that the "one-story disposition" of modernism was an exclusionary ethnocentric dynamic. The one story told was a Western tale that carefully excluded non-Western and female sagas from the chronicles of culture and art.

Affirmative postmodernists called for the art world to overcome this narrow cultural focus that erases the names of non-Western artists and relegates their work to an unconscious expression of cultural tradition. This postmodernist recognition was a critique of liberal racism and sexism that has permeated Western high culture despite claims of universal human rights, the sanctity of the individual and support of pluralism. Western racism, thus, is not simply the product of right-wing forces. Western artistic studies over the last century, for example, have consistently excluded most everything not white or bourgeois as scholars sought to tell the one coherent story of artistic progress. During the latter part of this era even "ethnic artists" who worked within European modernist traditions were viewed as "inauthentic" and "uninventive." If they chose to pursue so-called "ethnic art," they were relegated to the cultural gulag outside of the "story of art." This artistic catch-22, postmodernists proclaimed, was the work of progressives who prided themselves on their universals and lack of provincialism.

The postmodern artistic production that emerged from this bubbling cauldron of theoretical musings sought to transcend modernist elitism and conflate "high" and "low" cultural forms while concurrently embracing tradition and using it in playful and ironic ways. In this mode postmodernists used pastiche with its patchwork and collage of ideas and images. Often the ideas and images put together were ostensible opposites—old and new, "high culture" and "low culture," progressive and regressive, logical and illogical, Western and non-Western and "male" and "female" just to name a few. In such juxtapositions postmodern artists seemed to delight in the contradictions, chaos, asymmetry and jocularity that resulted. To deflate the egos of the heroic male modernist artists postmodernists in this same ludic spirit skewered their posturings of profundity, genius and "the maestro" (Wilson, 1993; Jordan and Weedon, 1995; Best and Kellner, 1991).

Embedded in this playful postmodern art are serious analytical themes that have profoundly influenced my own view of the relationships connecting art, culture, politics, cognition and education. In the pastiche of postmodern art one notes the creation of a context where improvisational interpretation can take place. In this crazy-quilt of juxtapositions, postmodern artists recontextualized images and concepts in ways that induced observers to contemplate the meaning of such relationships. In the affirmative postmodernist tradition such pastiche and eclecticism seem to point to a celebration of various cultural and artistic traditions around the planet and the insights that might come from examining them in relation to one another. Such traditions should be open to everyone regardless of background and all should learn from the various forms, techniques, concepts and values expressed in the diverse traditions.

Postmodern art carried a dada gene that permeated many of its productions. Indeed, some of the earliest postmodern work by Jasper Johns, Robert Rauschenberg and Andy Warhol were termed neo-dada by several art critics. The distancing from the grand tradition of art and the disdain of the affectations of bourgeoisie culture reflected the dadaist spirit and fanned the postmodernist attraction to appropriation, hyperirony and irreverence. In the context of our delineation between ludic and affirmative modes of postmodernism, more ludic artists rejected avant-garde concerns with social change while the more affirmative postmodern artists embraced them. Robert Rauschenberg's work, for example, illustrated numerous postmodern themes with his collages constructed from the debris of consumer society. Combining such "trash" with images from classical paintings and objects such as stuffed goats, Rauschenberg and many postmodern artists who followed him worked to produce an aesthetic of disharmony (Wilson, 1993; Cary, 1998; Best and Kellner, 1991).

High Above the Rest: The Cultural Politics of High-Low

In this disharmonious context Jasper Johns joined with Rauschenberg in the early 1960s to attack modernism's tendency to hold itself above popular culture. In this spirit Johns incorporated common consumer products in his collage paintings and made bronze sculptures with artifacts such as beer cans. Recognizable in the consciousness of such postmodern artists was a need to proclaim the death of the modernist avant-garde. The postmodernists wanted to make sure everyone understood that modernist avant-garde art was now part of the institutionalized and aesthetically inert status quo. It had become mere window dressing for consumerism. A new world was coming and the times were changing, the postmodernists announced, and they would not be so quick to place their work above more popular arts, above the productions of popular culture. The boundaries between "high art" and "low art" were beginning to fade.

As Karel Rose writes in her chapters here, understanding this high-low distinction and its aesthetic and cultural meanings were important issues in our team-taught course—and, thus, in this book. How do these labels evolve? Who designates these categories and distinctions? She asks. The issues I am working with in this chapter hold these questions as navigational instruments. What we are dealing with here are the complexities of cultural exchange. In any cultural and/or artistic negotiation individuals are operating in relation to many texts that play a role in the development of their identities and in the mode and content of their interactions with other people. These texts interact with an individual's past experience and present conditions. They typically involve matters of race, class, gender, sexuality, religion, ethnicity, geographical place and other factors. These dynamics constitute a process that have been labeled by scholars in the discipline of cultural studies as "cultural politics." The questions we have raised in this book and the issues we have explored can be referred to as the *cultural politics of art*.

As the high art of avant-garde modernism worked itself into a zone of safety and social accommodation, popular culture and the low art forms within it were gaining a new influence in U.S. culture. Radio and its promotion of rock music, television and its cultural power, the accelerating influence of advertising, comics and other pop cultural forms were assuming an unprecedented social prominence. Many people were gravitating to these forms as a visceral reaction against the pomp of high cultural production. Postmodern artists such as Warhol and architects such as Robert Venturi made use of public knowledges and popular artifacts and like Rauschenberg and Johns connected their art to the lived world of the era. These artists embraced a cultural politics suspicious of an art establishment that would separate great art from the commerce of the world in museums, institutes and galleries. Like many rebellious artists who came before them, they wanted to connect art to life in a variety of ways.

In the social context of the 1960s, entertainment was beginning to play a new and more prominent role in American life. To compete with popular culture forms and their entertainment value postmodern artists began to position themselves as entertainers. By the end of the twentieth century even high art itself would begin to position itself in this way—the Brooklyn Museum, for example, in the fall of 1999 promoted the Sensation exhibit in the spirit of a rock concert or a wrestling match. Art is not to be sequestered for the elite, postmodernists contended, it should be there for all people. High art roadblocks to the production, appreciation and benefits of art should be removed, postmodern artists argued, and more of the cultural interactions and productions that occur daily in numerous social spheres should be included in artistic and scholarly analyses. Since everyone is a cultural producer and receiver, the postmodernists were angered by the way high art promoters and their educational allies operated to exacerbate the sociocultural distance between the elite culture and that of common people. Contrary to the elitist pronouncements of critics such as Harold Bloom who argues that the greatest cultural productions cannot be understood by "common people," the early postmodern artists believed that most people can understand anything that grabs their interest. Nonetheless, with the establishment of postmodern art in the last three decades of the twentieth century and its increasing closeness to the financial establishment questions began to be raised about the elitism of postmodern art. Such art, the argument went, was merely the next form of art to gain canonization and, thus, enter the domain where it was bought and sold by the wealthy (Beyer, 2000; Wilson, 1993; Best and Kellner, 1991; Allen, 1995; Cowen, 1999).

Like its modernist avant-garde predecessor, postmodernist art—if this charge of elitism is accepted—has lost its ability to challenge the status quo with the shock of the unprecedented. In this context we can better understand why new York Mayor Rudi Giuliani's charge of elitism against the young British artists whose work was included in Sensation struck such a positive nerve with many "common people" around the city and the nation in general. Was he articulating in his crass appeal for conservative favor an unstated sense that postmodern artists and postmodern art were just the latest in the art historical pantheon to move from the popular domain to the realm of "high art?"

The 1990s and the early years of the twenty-first century with the powerful globalized economy and the Internet have been similar to the Gilded Age of the nineteenth century. Both periods have been marked by a great opportunity for those with capital to make phenomenal profits on the industrial economy of the nineteenth or the virtual economy of the late twentieth and early twenty-first centuries. In the nineteenth century the industrial profiteers—the so-called robber barons—made money on the art and artifacts they bought around the world. These tycoons built great American museums in which to store the art. In the contemporary era the new virtual money has also invested in all supported art, through the sponsorship of exhibitions—as with multimillionaire Charles Saatchi in the Sensation exhibit—or board members of museums who buy the art of those artists who show in their museums. This, of course, works to raise the value of their collections while promoting attendance at major shows. Once again the art world is in bed with big money and the cultural, political, aesthetic and educational effects of such intimacy will be interesting to dissect (Rorschach, 2000; Becker, 2000).

Making Sense of Art
Chutes and Ladders, Discourses and Canons

Traditional forms of art history and art education focus mainly on knowledge content, artifacts, and on who painted this and when did he paint it? What forms and techniques did he use that make the work significant? A more culturalist approach to art education and art history is also concerned with the nature of these disciplines themselves. When did they develop? Under what circumstances do they evolve? What role does power play in their everyday activities? A term used in cultural studies to signify this type of analysis of a discipline is "discourse." An understanding of discourse and discursive practices helps us appreciate the political (power-related) processes that shape what are assumed to be neutral disciplines, bodies of knowledge. When subjected to discursive analysis, the language and disciplinary assumptions of art history, for example, reveal a myriad of hidden and unexplored assumptions. Discursive practices involve the tacit rules that influence what can and cannot be said, who speaks and who must listen and whose depictions of reality are valid and worthy and whose are unlearned and unimportant.

These discursive inclusions and exclusions are typically quite subtle. In the cases of art history and art education, most observers are unaware of their operations. Indeed, suppositions thought to be harmless are exposed by cultural discourse analysis to be powerful political influences. High-art arbiters of quality operate as if they are oblivious to the ways their pronouncements, judgments and positionings of art/artifacts shape power relations between various groups of people—think of the previous examples of nonwhite, non-European art in avant-garde modernism. The privilege of the arbiters is hidden under assertions of quality and excellence, as particular cultural ways of being human and producing art are deemed superior to others. Museum directors, art dealers, wealthy sponsors and collectors, art critics and art professors have access to the status of arbiter and often work in this role to keep diverse voices and productions out of the picture.

By using discursive analysis, we gain a much more compelling insight into the cultural politics of art. We begin to uncover the ways the high-art establishment inscribes the superiority of whiteness, masculinity and Eurocentrism on art, art history, art criticism and aesthetics in ways that shape views of self and world. Just as discursive analysts have revealed hidden values defining the difference between normal and abnormal, sane and insane, good student behavior and disruptive student behavior, here we explore the veiled values constructing the difference between high and low art. The artful teaching of art education that we embrace wants to engage students in a higher-order understanding of the discursive dynamics of art. In many encounters with the educational arm of high art institutions, such discursive analysis seems to be positioned as an inappropriate behavior, a manifestation of not only bad pedagogy but, even worse, bad taste (Allen, 1995; Wilson, 1993).

Another discursive aspect of established art involves the nature of the history it produces. The heart of high-art history involves a focus on the great work of selected individuals and the movements they inspired. This Western single-story history, as postmodernists labeled it, proceeds chronologically without disruption, leading us intractably to the present. Discursive analysts are interested in who is left out of the story, the asymmetries that emerge, the power plays that oppress and, of course, the many other art stories to be told. In these discursive examinations of art history we begin to sense, for example, that what earns the label of artistic realism may be that work which is most faithful to the discursive rules of an official genre—not that which most accurately represents "reality." In this context we come to appreciate the notion that what appeared as realistic art to the arbiters of aesthetics in China during the Ming dynasty may constitute a profoundly different mode of painting than what was defined as realism in fifteenth-century France.

Thus, in our discursive analysis we begin to understand that what we view as the history of art, as great art or as realism is socially constructed by those with the power to decree. Art history as composed by the Western art establishment would not be recorded in the same manner in a society that did not place great value on fame and names. The discourse of official Western art history—a.k.a., art history—is a chronicle of cultural unconsciousness, of a blinding cultural narcissism. The "storage" of African, Caribbean, Asian and Native American art not in galleries but in anthropological museums is a material manifestation of the discursive practices of the Western art establishment. Defined by the discourse of Western art, such artifacts have not traditionally merited inclusion in art institutions; they are the primitive by-products of "the other."

The point that emerges here moves me to assert that the factors which produce impenetrable boundaries between "high art" and "low art" may be based not as much on carefully considered artistic qualities as on cultural, gender, racial and class biases. Non-Western art, women's art, art produced by individuals from the lower socioeconomic classes has been conveniently dismissed because of its failure to meet the discourse's "high standards of quality art."

"High art" and "low art," "good art" and "bad art" are not intractable categories that never change—they are constantly being renegotiated, perpetually in process, never at rest. Since they are discursively produced, they change when the discourse changes—and all discourses undergo change. My concern here is that we understand the negative impact of these discursive constructions and work to create new inclusive artistic traditions and innovative and multiculturally informed aesthetic practices. Such democratic and inclusive strategies are dedicated to naming and confronting the sexist, racist and class-biased pronouncements that travel under the banner of universal standards. Contrary to the way our democratic strategies are represented by the guardians of tradition as destructive of artist standards, such inclusive ways of studying art force the arbiters to examine the discipline from numerous perspectives, to understand a wide variety of artistic, cultural and interpretive traditions (Brown, 1995; Jordan and Weedon, 1995; Allen, 1995).

Understanding and acting on these dynamics raise the quality of art education, cultural analysis and the study of politics. Our insights are thickened and deepened by not only knowledge of aesthetic forms, techniques and perspectives but also by an awareness of the discursive dimensions delineated here. In the cognitive context created here we begin to gain the higher-order ability to see what is not present but yet is central to the entire process under examination. Seeing what is not there, we are prepared to go out and find it. Now that we know what we are looking for we begin to seek out long-subjugated art and not only include it in the curriculum but in the process learn from it. What, for example, do we learn from the attempts by our own art establishment to maintain its exclusion of art produced by artists from non-Western cultures from the universal history of art and to not subject their own discursive assumptions to analysis?

The Canonical View of Difference as Deficiency

As we ask these discursive questions and learn from the process of answering them, we encounter many revelations from many disciplinary domains. One art-related insight we gain involves the notion that it is problematic to equate the category of "high art" with "good art." The more accurate equation may connect "high art" with canonical art. The Western artist canon, the official story goes, consists of those officially sanctioned works of art that meet the criteria of strict rules of judgment. In the "Sensation" debate it was fascinating to read and listen to guardians of the canon react to the work of the young British artists. "They are challenging our tradition of quality," and "we are being assaulted by an invasion of barbarians," they cried. Artistic work that moves outside canonical boundaries must be contained, the priests of high art incant. In the process, of course, creativity, social critique and genuine forms of diversity are squashed (Ruesga, 1996; Walsh, 1999).

Indeed, difference has often been reduced to deficiency by the guardians of the artistic canon. The art of the other is seen only through the lenses of the canon. That which is artistically transgressive is "tamed" and rendered harmless by including it as a primitive stage of canonical development. The other is thus operating on a different (lower) rung on the evolutionary ladder. Once again as Westerners, we are reminded of our blessed superiority—a preeminence that gives us the right to establish the universal characteristics of "good art." The type of artistic analysis and art education called for here demystifies these hidden cultural and ideological dimensions of the canon. In this process it exposes not only what is excluded but also the ideological precepts shaping the inclusion of the other. In our cultural analyses of art we study the reasons that poor people, the "racially different," or women appear in particular ways in canonical work.

One of the most puzzling aspects of this picture of the high-art establishment involves the guardians' seeming inability to reflect on the forces that shape their aesthetic judgments. Are they unaware of the obvious impact of the ideology of Western colonialism on the fine arts? Many of their exhibitions, sponsored lectures and curricula would seem to indicate either a genuine or a cultivated lack of unawareness. In the twenty-first century it can no longer be simply stated that the West is white. England has an ever-increasing Caribbean population; Germany is home to many Turks; the United States has never been white but it is less white now than ever before. While the West is increasingly not white, Western high culture maintains its illusion of whiteness. But what would the Western artistic canon look like without its "appropriated" art—works stolen from Africans, Asians and indigenous peoples during colonization?

Often the colonial expeditions to bring back "primitive" art were financed by the art collectors and museum patrons themselves. These same agents were the ones who assessed the work, provided its "meaning," and distributed it to deserving collectors for sizable profits. Even as the guardians produced artistic scholarship on the "primitivism" of their colonial spoils, they failed to reflect on the ideological construction of their canon. Primitivism in art was conceptualized with a very simple but powerful schema: The artifacts of colonized peoples around the planet were objects placed on the low levels of the European artistic and cultural hierarchy. European artifacts—better known as art—occupied the higher rungs. Even in twenty-first-century artistic production, we see forms of neoprimitivism that while celebrating the art of the other still place artist and art at the bottom of the hierarchy.

A description of the ideological dimensions of the Western canon would not be complete without reference to its patriarchal foundations: the male artist as genius who constructs his own world and creates the rules by which it operates. This privilege was not granted to women or the racial other, only to the white male—the one with the entitlement to creative rebelling and the innovation it summoned. Says who? The white male guardians of the canon. *He* is the one who is heroic in his vision and electrifying in his aesthetic breakthroughs. It is hard for the guardians to express such sentiments about a female artist. The white male artistic hero is the artistic analyst who recognizes the formal aspects of artistic technique. Though "others" may have produced interesting artistic forms, it was the white man who discovered that they were of interest. Indeed, it is he that stands ahead of the aesthetic frontier: Balboa discovered the Pacific Ocean; Picasso discovered the "flat plane" of African art (Rorschach, 2000; Jordan and Weedon, 1995; Best and Kellner, 1991; Turner, 1996).

Making Sense of Art: Developing a Complex Hermeneutics of the Visual

In our discussion of high and low art—the analysis of "who says?" what is good and bad art and the examination of the way discursive and canonical factors shape the ways art is viewed—we have been studying the larger issue of interpretation. Hermeneutics involves the art of interpretation; the word is derived from the Greek god, Hermes, the messenger, who interpreted the pronouncements of the gods and delivered his readings to other gods and mortals. Interestingly, Hermes both clarified and played with these messages, in the process alerting humans to the ambiguity and complexity of the process of meaning making in everyday life. No matter how certain and direct an expert in art may be about the meaning of a particular painting or sculpture, a student or teacher who understands hermeneutics will know better. All narratives about the meaning of art are interpretations—and interpretations are never simple.

The interpretive act is tricky—Hermes was, after all, the "trickster god"—because a text to be interpreted, whether it be visual or print, can't be separated from meanings and inscriptions granted it by past, present and future meaning makers. For example, a Volkswagen may be a cute little lime green car, but it can never be completely separated from its Nazi origins as Adolph Hitler's people's car for the Third Reich. Thus, cuteness has an edge in the hermeneutics of Volkswagens. The hermeneutics advocated here is aware of the complexity of meaning making, of the effort to make sense of art, that no pristine interpretation exists. No form of art analysis or art criticism can claim a privileged position that enables the production of authoritative knowledge. Art critics like all other "knowledge producers" must always judge art in relation to something else in the world—in relation to an aesthetic theory, an art canon, a political system of meaning, a social theory, etc.

We are all—Karel Rose and myself included—shaped by these dynamics which, in turn, shape our views of art. We all see art in the world and make sense of it within the world's boundaries and blinders. Our purpose here is to bring to consciousness the ways our and other people's views of art are shaped by these boundaries and blinders. When we are aware of the forces that shape the ways art is viewed, we are able to provide more compelling insights into the nature of art and its relationships with the cultural, political, cognitive and educational domains. With these hermeneutical concepts in mind, we can move to new levels of aesthetic understanding. We can become smarter about both art and the world.

Hermeneutics, Art and Politics: The Shifting Sands of the Postmodern Landscape

At this point it is important to note that the process of aesthetic judgment, of making meaning in the artistic domain, is not some frill that relegates art to an isolated and rarefied plane of human activity. We are operating here in both the intrinsically valuable domain of art and also in the commerce and politics of the lived world. The process of interpretation, of meaning making is central to the cultural and political process; it shapes questions of justice and power and determines quality of life for the world's inhabitants. The cultural politics referenced previously is intimately tied to these hermeneutic issues. Cultural politics, simply stated, is a struggle over meaning and as such a contest it works to shape identities. A particular articulation of cultural politics wins a battle when a collection of individuals come to make meaning of art and other social texts in a particular way.

In the "Sensation" controversy, for example, various cultural politicians sought to engage individuals in interpreting the works in ways that resonated with their cultural politics. Were the productions filth, as Mayor Giuliani contended, or were they innovative works of art as maintained by Brooklyn Museum of Art director Arnold Lehman? The cultural politics of "Sensation" was not simply about how we view art but involved the way we make sense of the world, our moral, ethical and political sensitivities and how we view ourselves as human beings. This is why the controversy was so important in Karel's and my class: It illustrated the connections between art and life in a very concrete and explicit manner. Indeed, it brought the importance of the hermeneutics of art into a crystal-clear focus.

If we can enter into the study of art with these interpretive dynamics in mind, we can make connections with a variety of social, political and psychological domains that provide us with a much more mature and complex view of the world and ourselves. Social theorist Pierre Bourdieu (Dunn, 1998; Brown and Szeman, 2000) argues that the hermeneutics of art demands that we understand the relationship between art and power, the forces that have shaped the discourse of art criticism and the cultural context that has constructed the consciousness of those within the discipline of art. With benefit of these insights, he maintains, we are empowered to reflect critically on the social, cultural and political forces that shape us, our interpretations of art and our artistic productions. We become sophisticated analysts of cultural politics, an essential skill of citizenship in a postmodern era where political consciousness is more likely to be constructed in the cultural realm than on the traditional terrain of politics.

The postmodern era of the last thirty to forty years has witnessed an amazing political phenomenon—the death of the traditional political domain. Public political issues arouse much less passion than in previous eras in the United States. Issues concerning the improvement of the public sphere or social progress in areas of justice and the extension of the democratic process are viewed as irrelevant in the postmodern politics of cynicism, so why bother with them? A key understanding in this political domain that makes the meaning making process of cultural politics and the interpretation of art more important than ever involves the fact that the cultural domain has become the most important *political* arena. Areas that were once considered trivial venues of entertainment by political analysts are now used for profound political "education."

Thus, the cultural politics of art with its hermeneutics and meaning making shapes our political sensibilities. The mayor of New York inserts himself into a controversy ostensibly over art; presidential candidates discuss their favorite movies with Oprah; political organizations fight over the role of Hollywood in public life; the funding of art museums becomes a key issue in various political campaigns—the times they are a changing, *again*. Indeed, the questions we are raising here about what an artistic production means; what is "high art," "low art," "bad art," "good art," the questions "Sensation" raised about "immoral art" and "morally inspirational art" are profoundly contentious inquiries in the early twenty-first century. I don't think it hyperbole to argue that over the past 25 years these questions and questions like them concerning how aesthetic and artistic standards are determined with all their related moral, ethical and political implications have torn American society asunder (Jordan and Weedon, 1995; Dunn, 1998; Brown and Szeman, 2000).

Aesthetic Trespassing: Art, Interpretation and Context

The postmodern turn with its questions about the rules of artistic and authentic judgment was deeply resented by the guardians of artistic tradition. As postmodern analysts promoted the development of an interpretive distance or cultural arbiters and their constructions of aesthetic value, conservatives and traditionalists denounced such activities as markers of cultural and moral decline. Drawing upon the affirmative and democratic aspects of postmodernism, we promote a deeper understanding of artistic interpretation that engages the role of connections and contextualization in this complex process. Pushing the interpretive envelope and its intimate connection to the cultural, political, cognitive and educational, we maintain that context profoundly influences artistic evaluation as it shapes individuals' choices of what aspects of the world to connect to the domain of art.

Like hypertextual links on the Internet, what we connect to can dramatically affect our interpretation of a text. Context provides meaning to a work of art no matter how much the guardians may claim the essential form of the work determines its value. Thus, our aesthetic hermeneutics insists on the analysis of the context, the cultural circumstances of a work's production and reception and the ways these processes surrounding a work of art shape the political, cultural, educational and conceptual nature of our lives. With these hermeneutical insights and a focus on the context in which the artistic process takes place, we seek to promote a form of art analysis and art education that respects the complexity of the interrelationships connecting art to the political, cultural, educational and psychological domains. In this spirit we use the term *complex aesthetics*—a concept to be extended later in this chapter (Heck, 1998; Best and Kellner, 1991; Stossel, 1998; Allen, 1995; Kester, 1997).

With our notion of complex aesthetics we reconceptualize works of art education. In this reconceptualization works of art, art criticism, museums, patrons, art history and artists themselves are carefully viewed in their social, cultural, political and aesthetic contexts. Our original questions are seen in a new light as we come to view the historical circumstances surrounding the inclusion of a particular object and artist in the canon—equally important, of course, are the canonical exclusions. Here we ask with the benefit of context how such decisions related to the owners of canonized or excluded art and the social roles such artifacts have occupied over time. Of course, the artistic/aesthetic context created by Western colonialism is important to our complex aesthetics and the analytical concerns and education it supports. To understand the history of world art and Western art we cannot continue excluding the insights provided by a detailed awareness of the effects of Western colonialism.

Without such discernments official art studies continue to confuse a view of art filtered through colonialism with what the guardians refer to as "the story of art"—that is, the truth about art. Again they are unaware of the complex aspects of interpretation and fail to see the impact of Eurocentrism on their interpretive schemata. In the curriculum of complex aesthetics, for example, a rigorous historical analysis of the beginnings of European art's appropriation of non-Western art in the late nineteenth century and the cultural, political and economic forces connected to the cooption would be an important element of study. In this educational context we would spend significant time with students making sense of the influence of such intercultural encounters on not only art but on the subsequent political, cultural, social and educational character of the twentieth and now the twenty-first centuries.

What happened when European artists found that African, Native American and other indigenous forms of art played a different social role than did Western art? How did Western artists interpret the non-Western spiritual uses of art as incarnations of specters and deities with the power to shape everyday lives? How did indigenous artists and other community members interpret the activities of Western art "collectors" in their villages? How did these encounters affect the Westerners? The indigenous peoples? The indigenous works collected by the Western colonialists were for the most part relatively new pieces of art. They were represented as ancient pieces from the most "primitive" beginnings of human civilization. The hierarchical thinking embedded in such characterizations and its quick acceptance as truth by Westerners provide significant insights into European racial and self-conceptions at the turn of the twentieth century.

That official art history continues to perpetuate these colonialistic perspectives in the twenty-first century should be sobering to those concerned with the development of a complex aesthetics and issues of cultural and racial justice (Jordan and Weedon, 1995). Non-Western art is viewed as a trip to "a land that time forgot," "that civilization passed by." These artistic rides in the time machine bring us face to face with "wild men from Borneo" and the artifacts their "ancient" ancestors produced. It really doesn't matter when they were actually produced; because of the lack of cultural progress, contemporary artistic production is stuck in the same primitive mode. Many assume that great progress has been made in the West over the last few decades concerning cultural reflection about these manifestations of colonial representation. Unfortunately, however, a survey of exhibitions of non-Western art in American museums even in the past decade reveals an alternate story. Western artistic colonialism lives on in the twenty-first century.

Fecal Hermeneutics: Art, Interpretation and the African Other

During our "high art," "low art" class, Karel and I were fascinated by the way these hermeneutic questions about art and race emerged in the "Sensation" controversy. At the center of the controversy was artist Chris Ofili's painting, "The Holy Virgin Mary." Mayor Giuliani and many cultural conservatives had labeled the work as sacrilegious and an affront to all Catholics. Ofili's Virgin Mary is a black woman encircled by angels constructed by cut-out buttocks from pornographic magazines. Importantly, her breast is formed by elephant dung. It was the use of this medium in the painting that seemed to elicit such powerful reactions from observers in New York and around the country. Interpreting his own work, Ofili told observers that dung was a key element employed in many of his paintings to give them a sense of connection to the earth. In an interview with the *New York Times* he referenced the hermeneutic dimension of his artistic use of dung, pointing out that even though it is "incredibly simple," it elicits a variety of meanings and interpretations.

But dung, like many other materials, cannot be separated from the many inscriptions and meanings made of it in different cultures and different historical periods—contemporary U.S. culture not withstanding. Indeed, there are many cultural and historical meanings of dung—some Christian, some Western, some pantheist, some African, some indigenous, some scientific, and so forth. Needless to say, dung's meaning is in the eye of the perceiver and the constellation of meanings he or she culturally and historically brings to the observation. In the rural Tennessee fundamentalist Protestant world of my father, there was no way around it—dung, by whatever moniker, was dirty and references to it were vulgar. There was no cultural contingency here; fecal hermeneutics were clear cut and obvious no matter how dung might have been used in Africa. And in light of the cultural differences between my father's rural Protestant and Mayor Giuliani's urban Catholic mutual interpretation of the meaning of feces and African people's architectural and medicinal uses of the multiply inscribed substance, we begin to see the complexity of an intercultural hermeneutics of art.

Even among Africans themselves there was profound disagreement, with Christian Africans often taking issue with the fecal hermeneutics of those with more traditional African religious precepts. While there are profound exceptions to this breakdown, many Christian Africans argued that Africans have no special penchant for dung and that Ofili's work cheapened African-based art. Individuals with traditional African religious viewpoints seemed more inclined to interpret the painting's use of dung as a celebration of African culture. Thus, the context in which a perceiver operates, in this case transcending mere cultural location and involving religious orientation, exerts an impact on the way interpretation is made.

Others coming from specific academic theoretical traditions read other dynamics into Ofili's painting of the Virgin. Social theorist Coco Fusco, for example, employing a psychoanalytic art criticism contended that Ofili knew either consciously or subconsciously exactly what he was trying to do. By the use of dung in his paintings, she wrote, he was constructing an allegory about the place of black people and his own place as a black man in the contemporary world of art. Whether we buy Fusco's entire psychoanalytical interpretation or not, one point she raises cannot be discarded in a complex hermeneutics: Ofili's work cannot be removed from the inscriptions of meanings circulating around race in contemporary New York, U.S., Western and even global societies.

Ofili's race, the African and black cultural references of the painting, the explosive racial politics of New York at the time of the "Sensation" exhibit, Mayor Giuliani's controversial role in defending the New York police against charges of racism, the cultural and racial politics of the Brooklyn Museum as a bulwark of the European artistic canon in a racially diverse borough of New York City all generated a context for making sense of the racial significations of "Sensation" and "The Holy Virgin Mary." There was something combative about Ofili's painting viewed in such a highly charged interpretive context. Whether he consciously or unconsciously intended it or not, "The Holy Virgin Mary" walked into a spider web of racial significations and volatile racial emotions. Multiple meanings of such images were going to be made in New York City in the fall of 1999—investment in the hermeneutic racial economy was much too high. Ofili's significations of racial difference with his use of the African artistic technique of assemblage combining diverse elements and textures (dung, in particular) spontaneously combusted in the oxygen tent of Gotham semiotics (Consentino, 2000).

Art, Interpretation and Multiculturalism: Culturally Inscribed Meanings

All cultural entities and cultural behaviors are texts that derive their various meanings from the context(s) in which they are encountered. Stated another way, all textual meanings are socially constructed, not prearranged, fixed and absolute. Drawing upon our previous discussion of the "Sensation" exhibit, what is the transcultural, absolute meaning of dung? In light of the different social contexts from which we may view it—we come to appreciate the complexity of its meaning in general and in Chris Ofili's art, in particular (Allen, 1995). Thus, if meanings of cultural texts and in our case, works of art, are contextually dependent, then the possibility of challenging meanings that hold hurtful consequences, that construct racism, gender bias and class condescension exists. A complex aesthetics is grounded on this recognition and its ethical imperative to act. In the last three decades of the twentieth and the first decade of the twenty-first century, we have recognized that meanings of social texts in America have been shaped by a variety of factors. Race is particularly important in this context (Kincheloe, Steinberg, Rodriguez and Chennault, 1998; Rodriguez and Villaverde, 2000).

Particular ways of interpreting the world and its objects become dominant modes of seeing in specific cultural and historical settings. Based on power relationships between various racial and ethnic, gender and class groups, some interpretations come to seem as if they are more than mere opinions—they come to be viewed as commonsensical, even natural. In the first few centuries of the American experience the belief that African Americans and Native Americans were inferior, incapable of rational action was accepted as one of these "natural interpretations." With the civil rights movement of the mid-twentieth century, many of these "commonsensical" racial meanings were challenged, and the society engaged in a protracted debate over racial matters.

By the end of the 1960s many white Americans came to believe that the civil rights movement had "gone too far" and that the foundations of white supremacy were being challenged. New interpretations of race began to emerge in a variety of social, cultural, political, economic and educational spheres. Aaron Gresson (1995, 2002) labeled these new ways of making meaning as a form of "racial recovery"—in this case the effort to recover the perceived losses of the civil rights movement. In this recovery of white supremacy new ways of interpreting cultural objects began to arise. Contrary to overwhelming empirical evidence to the contrary, the new interpretations assumed that racial minorities had achieved greater power and opportunities for success than whites. African Americans, Latinos, Native Americans, Asian Americans and even women, the interpretation alleged, had gained an unwarranted privilege at the expense of white Americans, especially white males.

The omnipresence of the "recovery interpretation" produced and still produces white anger. Emerging from such an interpretation have been many texts that depict white Americans as a people under siege. Movies such as *Falling Down*, the *Lethal Weapon* series and the *Die Hard* series, for example, presented stories of white male rage and dissatisfaction (Allen, 1995). In this recovery context, consider Ofili's work in "Sensation." Did the sense of whites under siege, as the new victims of racism combined with the racial tensions sparked by the NYPD's shooting of African immigrant, Amadou Diallo and the brutal sodomizing of Haitian immigrant Abner Louima have an impact on New York City's conservative white community's reading of "Sensation"? Many conservative white New Yorkers felt the police were being persecuted because they were white men trying to control crime in the black community. Of all the work in the "Sensation" exhibit it was Ofili's painting of the African-inscribed, black Virgin Mary that elicited the most comment and outrage from conservative white New Yorkers and their spokesperson, Mayor Giuliani.

Would the painting have elicited such vitriolic reactions in another cultural context and another time? The racial politics of New York City in the fall of 1999 combined with the larger white recovery context, I contend, profoundly shaped the meaning of Ofili's "The Holy Virgin Mary, as it was exhibited at the Brooklyn Museum. In our socially constructed context we understand that the painting did not simply *have a meaning*. Even Ofili's explanation of its meaning in terms of connecting the image of the Virgin Mary to the earth is somewhat irrelevant in relation to the socially constructed interpretations of the work. Indeed, Ofili may have produced the work, but he lost control of its meanings as soon as the painting entered the highly charged and socially inscribed political, cultural and racial context of New York City in the fall of 1999.

Jungle Boogie: Meaning Is on the Lam

As Maxine Greene (1988, 1995) has frequently argued, if a work of art is to have meaning, individuals viewing it give it meaning. In this constructivist context artistic meaning is created in the interaction of the act of viewing, the work of art and the world. Since the world and the viewer are always in a process of changing, the interpretations of a work that are constructed will always change. Thus, in the case of Ofili's "The Holy Virgin Mary," those who view the painting, for example, in the year 2017 or in Japan, may provide a significantly different interpretation of it than their end-of-century New York counterparts. Operating in a different social context, they may look back at the reaction of many New Yorkers to the painting as bizarre and difficult to comprehend.

This argument, of course, flies in the face of the view of art and aesthetic criticism delivered daily by the guardians of high art. In this effete context artistic meaning exists behind glass and is guarded against upstarts with divergent ways of discerning the meaning of such cultural treasures. A complex aesthetics is interested in art as it is viewed in changing contexts and in diverse cultural climates. I am interested in watching, for example, what happens to Ofili's "The Holy Virgin Mary" over the coming decades. Will it still elicit such emotion? Will it fade into artistic obscurity? Will it become a classic? Will it take on new meanings and significance for a new generation? No one knows for sure, but we can safely predict that its status and interpretation will change.

An example of an earlier racially inscribed work of art might help extend our analysis of culture, race and artistic interpretation. In 1943 Wilfredo Lam produced a painting entitled, "The Jungle," that attempted to celebrate the spiritual energy of primitivism in lieu of Western modernism. Lam wanted to proclaim the power of Africa and the Africanized Caribbean and its value for Westerners alienated by their culture's hyperrationalization, urbanization and despiritualization. Typical descriptions of the painting reference its primitive vision of nature marked by deep greens and blues and body parts shaded with browns and oranges. Observers wondered where plant life ended and human life began in "The Jungle," as they observed green plants with female breasts, bamboo shoots with hands and/or feet and faces where there could be flowers. As he rejoiced in these images, Lam confided that Western "progress" beyond this primal state of being was not really progress at all.

In 1943 and the years immediately following the debut of "The Jungle," many avant-garde, progressive critics celebrated the racial liberalism of the work. As Lam argued, he wanted to shock the racial oppressors with his bold primal images. But as the world changed and colonized peoples around the world began to revolt against Western domination, Lam's painting began to be interpreted differently. The only way Lam provides Westerners to recover from the ravages of their cultural elitism is through an encounter with primitivism in the African jungle. And such a move, many non-Western and nonwhite critics insisted, is dangerous as it associates African people with a primeval state that removes them from modernity.

Lam, like so many others before and after him, held a simplistic view of interpretation. If he said the painting was meant as a celebration of the genius of Africanness, then that would be the way others would make sense of it. But, as we know, meaning making is not that simple. By the last three decades of the twentieth century, Lam's association of Africanness with primitivism was seen as giving aid to racist agendas that relegated black people and their culture(s) to an inferior position. The painting had come to be viewed as an affront to people of color, a stereotyped view of the African "other." Lam, despite his progressive intentions, could not control the meaning of "The Jungle." As some observers have commented, the slaveowners of the nineteenth-century Americas would probably have enjoyed Lam's painting—much to his horror and disbelief (Padgham, 1988; Allen, 1995; Jordan and Weedon, 1995).

Transgressive Hermeneutics: Resisting Analytical Closure

A complex hermeneutics uses "The Jungle" to teach an important lesson about the artistic domain: beware of a final pronouncement of textual meaning. Such a position opens a possibility of resistant readings of art, even high canonized art, that edify not only our aesthetic sensibilities but our cultural and political understandings as well. Many avant-garde artists of the 1960s understood this dynamic, as they worked to bring the audience and its meaning-making ability into their artwork. Robert Rauschenberg asked the audience to help make sense of his so-called white paintings as they were subjected to various shadowing and lightings. John Cage often rebelled against the imposition of meaning by artists from diverse media, insisting that his audiences participate in determining the meaning of his music. Such conceptual moves successfully highlighted both the importance and complexity of a hermeneutics of art.

In this recognition of complexity single views of canonicity are subverted; patriarchal and Western artistic exclusions are confronted and the diverse and often hidden forces that construct artistic meaning are exposed. Learning from a variety of non-Western and indigenous cultural knowledges, the complex hermeneutics of art taking shape here is concerned with the way artistic analysis takes place without adequate examination of its own values, assumptions and discursive rules. Indeed, such a way of viewing, studying, helping produce and teaching about art refuses to bow its head in the presence of the authority of the guardians of tradition. This emerging complex aesthetics stakes no exclusive claim to the domain of expertise. It simply and humbly offers these ideas and analytical processes for consideration in the emporium of artistic interchange (Wilson, 1993; Benshoff, 1999).

Such transgressive acts of artistic and political analysis are essential to the emerging global society and contemporary American society. The United States has not yet come to terms in the first decade of the twenty-first century with the fact that it is not simply a white Eurocentric nation. The nation's social and cultural institutions, for example, do not operate on the appreciation that very shortly the majority of American citizens will not be classified as white. Where exactly does women's, African American and indigenous art fit into the pantheon of white male art? How is American society going to deal with that question and all of the other similar questions arising in related cultural, social, economic and political domains? These are the great questions of our time, despite the fact they are being successfully repressed in the cultural commerce of everyday life.

As usual, Maxine Greene (1988) puts it well when she maintains that the dictates of democracy demand that the world of art and art education open themselves to "voices seldom heard before." Such previously excluded artists can provide fresh insights into the ways Americans structure their experiences and interpret their everyday lives. This refers to the importance of seeking out and attending to multiple points of view. Such action helps us invalidate efforts to end the dialogue about canonicity, as we come to understand that no disciplinary analysis can ever be complete. There is always another perspective to consider, another way of seeing that makes our previous certainty seem naive, parochial. The power of subjugated knowledges in all domains, in this context the artistic sphere, provides hope in its delineation of what is *not* present and what is still left to be represented, said, referenced and exposed.

In this domain of inclusivity, multiple voices and diverse ways of making meaning we can all feel good about our generous sprit, our effort to bring the excluded into the discourse of art and art criticism. A complex aesthetics, however, understands that such liberal self-congratulation is premature, that the question of inclusivity and analytical openness is far more complex than previously assumed. Many who read this work will possibly assert that the contemporary art establishment is not racially or ethically exclusive—indeed, many will argue, there's too much nonwhite, "ethnic" art being shown. It is true that throughout the twentieth century "artists of color" have been included in many artistic contexts. The question that is central to our efforts to make sense of art and its relation to the cultural, political, cognitive and educational domains concerns more the *conditions* of the incorporation of African, African American, Latino, Asian, Native American art and other "ethnic" work into Western institutions and disciplinary configurations.

A transgressive hermeneutics of art, a complex aesthetics is concerned in this "inclusionary context" with the way nonwhite artists and their art are reduced to ethnic artists and ethnic art. Such a process of otherizing removes them from the universal artistic narrative, coldly relegating them to the separate domain of the particular. And while their work may be extolled, it is honored "in its place"—as cilantro in the pico de gallo, spice in the entree, entertainment to break the monotony of the established. What is being referenced here is the "exoticization of the other," a process that has reached new heights in the last two decades. Such an exoticization is a new more complex form of racism that seductively whispers, I want you as it limits the way the racial other is understood: the tragic magic of the sensual, the physical and the emotional. You can be like Mike as long as you buy my Nikes. What emotional power Chris Ofili's work possesses, as he taps into the primitive animism of his African ancestors. Jungle fever. This neoracism of exoticization determines racial abilities, thus limiting possibility (Jordan and Weedon, 1995).

Struggling with the Aesthetic: Avoiding Reductionism

As we now realize, aesthetic questions are sticky. Even the definition of aesthetics eludes attempts for simplicity. Having alluded to the notion of a complex aesthetics, I will not attempt to be more specific about the meaning of such a concept. In his thoughtful book, *Critical Art Pedagogy: Foundations for Postmodern Art Education*, Richard Cary (1998) writes of the complexity of the word "aesthetics."

> The word "aesthetics" appears often in everyday speech. Most people use it with some degree of confidence to refer to a set of meanings revolving loosely around the idea of attractive appearance. Integrated within the art world, these various meanings center on the engaged personal experience of attraction or appeal an individual feels while encountering the art object or phenomenon semantically, intellectually and emotionally. As a result of an encounter, one decides whether the art object or phenomenon is aesthetically appealing and hence, whether it

> possesses aesthetic value. We tend to think of the "amount" of aesthetic value as a function of the degree of attractiveness. (If this everyday usage seems circular, it is because it is circular.) (p. 270)

Of course, aesthetics has something to do with questions of beauty, pleasure, art, music, poetry and feeling. Furthermore, as Cary maintains, it involves the relationship of these dynamics to the analysis and discursive shaping of art and the nature of human interaction with art. Landon Beyer (2000) contends that aesthetic experiences involve a focus on both humanly produced objects of art and naturally created phenomena that possess qualities that engage us. Central to these understandings of the nature of aesthetics is the knowledge that individuals for thousands of years have debated what exactly constitutes the nature of aesthetic experience and how exactly art and aesthetic encounters should be understood. The relationship of the domain of aesthetics to other spheres of human endeavor has also been debated throughout history.

In the Western art establishment of the past few centuries, aesthetics has been closely associated with beauty viewed in terms of harmony and order. In this context beauty was seen as a universal good that was to be pursued as an end in itself. It didn't seem to occur to the guardians of the artistic tradition that in certain contexts beauty might be viewed as offensive. In times of tragedy, war or social strife, for example, an artist's dissolution of art's ties to the political, social, economic, ethical or moral domains in the pursuit of beauty might be viewed as an act of insensitivity. Traditional Western canonical perspectives on aesthetics consistently operated to limit the concerns of aesthetics, to contain it in the rarefied air of high art and remove it from the lived world of social commerce.

Drawing upon Cary's notion of critical aesthetics in our effort to avoid reductionism and to define a complex aesthetics, we seek a mode of engagement with art that refuses to position aesthetics as a series of non-negotiable facts and approaches to art and artistic judgment. In a complex aesthetics the rules of artistic criticism, analysis, production and social meaning are always open, always in process of changing, expanding and growing. The expansion and growth in this context takes place in the relationship between art and life. Indeed, a complex aesthetic is interested first in life and art's relationship to it. Art in this situation alerts us to the world; John Dewey argued that aesthetic experience should be reintegrated into the normal process of living. This Deweyan reintegration process is central to a complex aesthetics as it helps us understand the interrelationship of various domains of experience, especially the connection among art, a continuing education and life itself.

As historians of art have in the light of contemporary artistic debates generated by many of the issues referenced here reexamined the historical origins of the term aesthetics, they have uncovered some interesting insights. In early Greek philosophy, for example, many scholars located the aesthetic realm at the intersection of one's private body and its sensations with the so-called body politic. In this insight we discern an early articulation of our notion of a complex aesthetics that appreciates the complexity and social constructedness of the aesthetic realm. Indeed, as argued here, dominant culture and the power it exerts play a key role in understanding the ways aesthetic experience, high and low art and good and bad taste are defined. Aesthetics cannot be abstracted from social and political processes, reduced to form and technique, or separated from the larger dynamics of material (economic) production.

Thus, the foundation of a complex aesthetics rests on the understanding that the aesthetic is not a separate domain or an abstract realm—it is an integral aspect of life and the educational act. As such aesthetics, social awareness, ethical sensitivity and transformative action are inseparable, as artistic knowledge and experiences move us to see alternative manifestations of what could be, political critique of accepted institutional arrangements and empathy into the hurt and damage of oppression. As Karel Rose writes in this volume, such connections are central to the aesthetic experience and should be drawn on in the educational domain to connect the outside world to the classroom. Making these connections seamless is important to the creation of a rigorous and engaged pedagogy. Such an education helps students gain the intellectual and emotional insight necessary to the task of challenging racism, gender bias, class discrimination and homophobia (Brown, 1995; Heck, 1998; Kester, 1997; Beyer, 2000).

Like the surrealists, a complex aesthetician believes in the revolutionary potential of art. As art transforms political consciousness, it leads to awakened individuals who can change the world and use the social and cognitive power of difference to gain new perspectives on the human impact of existing social arrangements. But learning from the mistakes of transformative agents such as the surrealists, advocates of a complex aesthetics develop a far more sophisticated view of power and the ways it can reestablish social hierarchies even in the midst of revolutionary activity. These sociocognitive and political aspects of art and aesthetic experience are not commonly understood in United States society or education. The assumption of a complex aesthetics that an interconnected art raises complicated issues and highlights often suppressed perspectives is often met with befuddlement by the public in general and students in particular. Why are they displaying these works? they ask. Why don't they just paint some pretty pictures (Jordan and Weedon, 1995; Becker, 2000)?

Power Aesthetics: Gaining Authority

All aesthetic activity involves the previously discussed process of making meaning—and all meaning-making processes involve power. A complex aesthetician is especially interested in the way individuals and organizations gain the authority to provide the official version of what a work of art means. In this power context a complex aesthetician explores art history in a way that gets beyond a chronological account of the works of great men. Such a transformed art historian searches for the asymmetries, contradictions and erasures of canonical history, as he or she attempts to uncover the hidden power dynamics that shaped the official story. As one interested in culture, one who is fascinated by the relationship between art and life, I promote an aesthetic power consciousness that grants art the social importance it merits.

Art history, criticism and production and aesthetics are central forces in constructing and perpetuating prevailing ways of seeing the world. Thus, the power of the artistic and aesthetic domain involves not simply art but cultural politics in general. Art shapes us; aesthetics makes us who we are. As we have seen in regard to the racial aspects of modern art, the relative power relations between different cultural groups affect the nature of art, but art contributes to the perpetuation and extension of these asymmetrical relationships. The self-representations of non-Western peoples who had been colonized by Westerners were excluded by Western agents of the artistic canon with the power to dismiss such "primitivism." Such guardians of artistic tradition validated the work of Western artists who delineated their own representations of African, Asian and indigenous exoticism, eroticism and emotion.

The point in this contest that is so important to a complex aesthetics involves the power of Western arbiters to present a hierarchy of cultures and their artistic production. Power shapes the consciousness of both those who exercise it and those who have it exercised on them. In the case of Westerners, the authority to designate good and bad art as well as cultural worth in general has created a disturbing sense of privilege and entitlement. The Western self-concept, in fact, cannot be understood without an acknowledgment of the way Westernness has been defined in relation to non-Westernness with all the positive and negative binarisms that attend this depiction. The power relations of this cultural dualism have been so formidable that even well-intentioned artists could not escape its gravity. Works such as "The Jungle," for example, that attempted to celebrate non-Westernness ended up reifying the cultural hierarchy. No wonder the Western powerbrokers of art were not frightened by modernist avant-gardism (Jordan and Weedon, 1995).

In the context created by a critical aesthetics, it is totally understandable that the young British artists of "Sensation" should have sought innovation, disrespect for the canon and even shock. Indeed, Karel and I can understand that many of those who proclaimed the exhibit "sick and disgusting" were in part responsible for the "sick and disgusting" racism, poverty, class bias, gender bias and homelessness of contemporary life in their unwillingness to confront such travesties. Those disgusted by "Sensation" often come from the ranks of those wielding power in contemporary New York city and New York State. In the power analysis of a complex aesthetics, I would maintain that the "Sensation" artists were operating in a political context shaped by the influence of economic globalization on Britain over the last couple of decades.

These economic changes have worked to disempower many British young people by exacerbating social inequality and the rule of the free market. An examination of many of the pieces of the show reveals the sting of this political process. At the same time, however, there is no attempt to explain it, to bring together artistic, aesthetic, historical and social analysis for the purpose of providing insight into the malicious power dynamics at work. While in no way do I want to dismiss the importance of artists expressing anger and disillusionment in their work, a critical aesthetics with its power consciousness nudges artists to name oppression, power asymmetries and destructiveness. After identifying these dynamics, it is important that artists operating within the context of a critical aesthetics use their creative abilities to address these sociocultural pathologies.

I don't sense in "Sensation" a flood of compassion for the marginalized, a possibility for change in their situation or a future vision of what could be. Reading "Sensation" from the perspective of a critical aesthetician, I find the show fascinating, iconoclastic and filled with striking images. As I celebrate these dynamics, I am nevertheless left a little hollow by the celebration of the superficial, the absence of cultural and aesthetic history, the lack of social analysis and the vacuum left by the ignoring of power. Does all great art demand the inclusion of such features? Probably not. But in the context of a complex aesthetics, artists do need to deal with these dynamics on some subjective level (Walsh, 1999).

Through "Sensation"'s striking images of eviscerated cows and dysfunctional families, I come back to "The Holy Virgin Mary." It still stands out as one of the few pieces that moves us to new levels of commentary and analysis. None of these comments are meant in any way to detract from the social importance of the exhibit: the phenomenal juxtapositioning of "Sensation" with the racial climate of New York in the fall of 1999 created an unprecedented planetary alignment in art. As such, fascinating social, cultural, political, cognitive, educational and aesthetic dynamics swirled around it. Understanding all of this in the context of the commodification of contemporary artistic production, the exhibit raises questions in these domains that will occupy us for a long time.

A Complex Aesthetics and Cognition: Pursuing New Realms of Human Being

A great piece of art in the context of a complex aesthetics moves us to see anew, to move beyond common ways of viewing an entity, to make new connections, to interpret the world in new ways. What we are referencing here is cognition, the nature of our thinking. In this domain we begin to peer into even more aspects of the relationship between art/aesthetics, culture, politics, cognition and education. In these interrelationships we set out on a journey to discover the types of thinking that art makes possible. Operating in this way we make, in Maxine Greene's words, "a new commitment to intelligence" (1988, p. 126). Consider the nature of the complex relationship that connects these divergent domains and how this new commitment to intelligence, and, I would add, social justice is achieved.

As we study art, art criticism and our notion of a complex aesthetics with its concern with art's connection to life, we begin to enhance our intellectual abilities. In Karel and my course on "high art" and "low art" and the relations between these concepts and the "Sensation" exhibit, we worked to help students make connections in these domains that led to cognitive growth. As we discussed various ways of using, producing and judging art, we began to uncover the close connection between these dynamics and cultural context. As a result we realized that in a complex aesthetics, learning about art cannot take place outside of rigorous cultural analysis. The criteria for artistic evaluation in a particular context can always be traced on some level to parallel currents in the larger culture.

In the "Sensation" affair, for example, we could clearly see reflections of the passionate reactions to the artistic works in the "cultural war" taking place in New York in particular and the United States in general at the end of the twentieth century. There was no way to understand "Sensation" and the spectacular reaction to it without an appreciation of the cultural struggle between those who believed our culture was being debased by filth and lowbrow aesthetic production and those who maintained that U.S. culture was retreating to Eurocentric, patriarchal and elitist perspectives valued as universal and unquestionable truths. Such insights provided students windows into not only the construction of their own consciousness but a new understanding of the political domain.

In this situation they began to gain a more textured perspective not only on the political currents of the day and where they stood in relation to them but on the nature of power and its connection to cultural politics and artistic evaluation. Art like other cultural phenomena does not exist in a power vacuum. It, like other artifacts, is shaped by dominant and subordinate forms of power and gains its meanings only in this political context. Students began to discern the various ways power relations shaped the meanings "Sensation" assumed in the larger society. An art education that understands these aesthetic, cultural and political interrelationships can never be the same. It can never retreat to slide shows of canonical works with a unidirectional, decontextualized delineation of what a particular work means to students—students who, by the way, simply memorize such data and spit it back to the teacher on an "objective" test.

This, of course, is not the artful teaching that Karel and I are writing about. Such canonical imposition stupidifies rather than enlightens, closes off rather than opens up possibilities and undermines any larger commitment to intelligence. Indeed, this commitment to intelligence involves the cognitive dimension of our constellation of interconnections—art/aesthetics, culture, politics, education and cognition. It is on this cognitive dynamic that we now focus our attention. A basic cognitive dimension of art involves the ability of aesthetic experience to empower individuals to attend to that which was previously missed. In this manner individuals become cognizant of those elements and especially those relationships that elude everyday perceptions. As their eyes, ears, modes of analysis, intuitions, ways of seeing are attuned to the unseen, students and teachers gain a thicker view of the world and a deeper understanding of themselves (Cary, 1998; Greene, 1988).

In my own cognitive experience I was always infatuated by the consciousness-expanding power of surrealist art. In the surrealist context, art provided glimpses of alternative rationalities more like the cognitive processes of a dream experience than formal analysis. Instead of proceeding by linear argument derived from empirical facts or logical principles, surrealistic cognition employed metaphorical modes of analogy that operated to recast experience in an emotional/affective context. In this manner new ways of conceiving and interpreting scholarly concepts and everyday life were constructed that in my case directly led to new articulations of cognitive theory. See my work on postformalism (Kincheloe, 1993; Kincheloe and Steinberg, 1993; Kincheloe, Steinberg and Tippins, 1999; Kincheloe, Steinberg and Hinchey, 1999; Kincheloe, Steinberg and Villaverde, 1999).

Addressing the Complexity: Surrealist Insights and a Cubist Cognition

Viewing scholarly concepts and everyday life from the vantage point of surrealist art allows us to take the numbingly familiar and make it strange. In its new strangeness we begin to discover what was previously not present to our perception. Such insights recast the meaning of the experience in a new light. One of the reasons we use the term *complex*, as in a complex aesthetics, is that the more we understand about the world, the more complex it appears to be. In this recognition of complexity we begin to see multiple causations and the possibility of differing vantage points from which to view a phenomenon. It is extremely important to note at this juncture that the context from which one observes an entity shapes what he or she sees. The set of assumptions or the system of meaning making the observer consciously or unconsciously employs shapes the observation.

This assertion is not some esoteric, academic point—it shapes art, art criticism, artistic production, art education, social analysis and political perspectives. Acting upon this understanding, advocates of a complex aesthetics realize that art, aesthetic theory, cultural artifacts and the art curriculum hold more within them to be analyzed than first impressions sometimes reveal. In this sense different frames of reference produce multiple interpretations and multiple realities. The mundane, the everyday and the aesthetic dimension are multiplex and continuously unfolding—while this is taking place, human interpretation is simultaneously constructing and reconstructing their meaning. This is a complex situation, and all of us need to understand it as such (Lincoln and Guba, 1985;

Denzin and Lincoln, 2000; Briggs and Peat, 1989; Slaughter, 1989; Kincheloe, 2001).

A complex aesthetics promotes a spatial distancing from reality that allows an observer diverse frames of reference. The distancing may range from the extremely distant like astronauts looking at the earth from the moon, to the extremely close like Georgia O'Keeffe viewing a flower. At the same time, a complex aesthetician values the intimacy of an emotional connectedness that allows empathetic passion to draw knower and known together. In the multiplex, complex aesthetic view of reality, Western modernist linearity often gives way to simultaneity, as texts become a kaleidoscope of images filled with signs, symbols and signifiers to be decoded and interpreted. William Carlos Williams illustrated an understanding of such complexity in the early twentieth century as he depicted multiple, simultaneous images and frames of reference in his poetry. Williams attempted to poetically interpret Marcel Duchamp's *Nude Descending a Staircase*, with its simultaneous, overlapping representations serving as a model for what a complex aesthetician might label a cubist cognition.

Teachers who pursue the artful teaching that Karel Rose describes understand these concepts. Such educators work to extend their students' cognitive abilities, as they create situations where students come to view the world and disciplinary knowledge from as many frames of reference as possible. In a sense the single photograph of Cartesian thinking is replaced by the multiple angles of the holographic photograph. Energized by this cubist cognition, teachers informed by a complex aesthetics come to understand that the models of teaching they have been taught, the definitions of inquiry with which they have been supplied, the angle from which they have been instructed to view intelligence, the modes of learning that shape what they perceive to be sophisticated thinking and the ways that art has been represented to them, all reflect a particular vantage point in the web of reality.

Like reality itself, schools and classrooms are complex matrices of interactions, codes and signifiers in which both students and teachers are interlaced. Just as a complex aesthetics asserts that there is no single, privileged way to see the world, there is no one way of representing the world artistically, no one way of teaching art, no one way of writing art history. Once teachers escape the entrapment of the guardians of art and their monocultural, one-truth way of seeing, they come to value and thus pursue new frames of reference in regard to their students, classrooms and workplaces. In this cubist spirit, teachers begin to look at lessons from the perspectives of individuals from different race, class, gender and sexual orientations. They study the perspectives their African American, Latino, white, poor and wealthy students bring to their classrooms. They are dedicated to the search for new perspectives.

Drawing upon a complex aesthetics in this cognitive and pedagogical pursuit, these educators, like liberation theologians in Latin America, make no apology for seeking the viewpoints, insights and sensitivities of the marginalized. The way to see from a perspective differing from that of the guardians involves exploring an institution such as Western art from the vantage point of those who have been marginalized by it. In such a process subjugated knowledges once again emerge allowing teachers to gain the cognitive power of empathy—a power that enables them to take pictures of reality from different vantage points. The intersection of the vantage points allows for a form of analysis that moves beyond the isolated, decontextualized and fragmented analysis of modernist reductionism.

Cognitively empowered by these multiplex perspectives, complexity-sensitive educators seek a multicultural dialogue between Eastern cultures and Western cultures, a conversation between the relatively wealthy Northern cultures and the impoverished Southern cultures and an intracultural interchange among a variety of subcultures. In this way, forms of knowing, representing and making meaning that have been excluded by the modernist West move us to new vantage points and unexplored planetary perspectives. Understandings derived from the perspective of the excluded or the "culturally different" allow for an appreciation of the nature of justice, the invisibility of the process of oppression, the power of difference and the insight to be gained from a recognition of divergent cultural uses of art that highlight both our social construction as individuals and the limitations of monocultural ways of meaning making (Dobrin, 1987; Mandell, 1987; Talbot, 1986, 1991; Welch, 1991; Bohm and Peat, 1987; O'Sullivan, 1999; Kincheloe, Steinberg and Hinchey, 1999).

Taking advantage of these complex ways of seeing, a whole new world is opened to us. As cognitive cubists, teachers, students, artists, art critics and cultural analysts all come to understand that there always multiple perspectives. No conversation is over, no discipline totally complete. The domain of art is best equipped to teach this concept, as it exposes new dimensions of meaning, new forms of logic unrecognized by the sleepwalking dominant culture. As a cognitive wake-up call, art can challenge what Herbert Marcuse (1955) called "the prevailing principle of reason" (p. 185). In this context we come to realize that art and other aesthetic production provide an alternate epistemology, a way of knowing that moves beyond declarative forms of knowledge.

Literary texts, drama, music, dance, sculpture and painting empower individuals to see, hear and feel beyond the surface level of sight and sound. These aesthetic forms can alert individuals to the one-dimensional profiles of the world promoted by reductionistic researchers and art critics. Herbert Marcuse of the Frankfurt School of Critical Theory was acutely aware of this cognitive dimension of art and linked it to what he called a critical politics. Art assumes its liberating value, he wrote, when it is viewed in light of specific historical conditions. Thus, for Marcuse aesthetic transcendence of repressive social and cultural reality is a deliberate political act that identifies the object of art with the repressive social situation to be transcended. This, of course, is what I was attempting as we explored the racial dynamics of modernist avant-garde art and the ideological forces operating in that context.

Following Marcuse's arguments and the sociopolitical concerns of a complex aesthetics does not mean the promotion of art as propaganda for a particular point of view. This would be a misguided and disastrous interpretation of the ideas promoted here. Engaging in a critical aesthetics does not mean following a blueprint for sociopolitical action—instead it implies the opposite. It does seek justice but is always attuned to new perspectives on what this might mean and how the well-intentioned pursuit of justice may unintentionally oppress particular groups and individuals. To lessen these possibilities a complex aesthetics promotes a rigorous self-reflection and self-criticism. It is obsessively concerned with the ways our consciousness is constructed and our worldviews are formed and how these dynamics shape our interactions.

Thus, a complex aesthetics embraces an art and artistic analysis and criticism that illuminates the problematic, as it constructs new concepts, new angles from which to view the world. In this way, art with its producers, critics, cultural analysts, historians and educators gives birth to new meanings, as it breaks through the surface to explore the submerged social, political and aesthetic relationships that shape events. When it takes such dynamics seriously, education and the artful teaching that emerges in this context are characterized by acts of defamiliarization. An education grounded on a complex aesthetics seeks not only to defamiliarize the commonsense worlds of students but to create situations where student experience can be used to defamiliarize the world of schooling.

In this form of education educators employ artistic concerns with the "now" to defamiliarize the modernist school's unfortunate tendency to functionalize the role of instruction and to join with students to seek pleasurable ways of remaking the institution in line with a respect for intelligence. Overcoming the educational tyranny of an exclusive bourgeoisie reliance on delayed gratification and the mistrust of pleasure that accompanies it, teachers operating in the zone of complexity promote cognitive abilities unbowed by the mystifying power of the given. Emerging from this playful haughtiness is the realization that the arts can promote a form of teaching that requires interpretation and a form of thinking that seeks new experiences that facilitate interpretation. Such interpretation, Maxine Greene (1988) writes, exposes the forces that suppress "the spheres of freedom to which education might some day attend" (p. 130) (Bronner, 1988; Adler, 1991; Kincheloe, 2001).

Thus, cognitive cubism produces a multidimensional form of knowledge that is always open to new interpretations in its hermeneutical connection to larger processes. Such knowledge can never be final because it cannot control the differing contexts within which it will be encountered. In this absence of interpretive closure a complex aesthetics moves understanding away from reductionism into a more complex realm. This cognitive vis-à-vis hermeneutic dynamic reflects Karel Rose's concern with multiple ways of knowing and their ability to help students appreciate their own imaginations, creativities and intelligences. When we rely on particular ways of knowing usually associated with modernist linearity and positivism, teachers and art teachers in particular, operate in a manner that teaches students—particularly those who see the previously unseen—that they are capable.

The guardians of tradition both in the aesthetic and the cognitive domains are uncomfortable with admitting outsiders into the community of the "cultured" or the fraternity of the "intelligent." This multiple-ways-of-knowing idea is dangerous, they argue, because such openness is the first step down the dangerous road to a loss of standards. The only cognitive and educational alternative to this subversion of standards, the guardians maintain, is a unyielding protection of official ways of seeing and the certified canon of "true art." In this context, those of us who point to the boundaries and limitations of Western logical thought and its tendency for domination, ethnocentric arrogance and brutality are often faced with the anger and revenge of the guardians. Our call in our complex aesthetics to not only include previously marginalized art and its ways of seeing in the aesthetic canon but to bring these aesthetic/cognitive/political/educational perspectives to the effort to rethink the nature of aesthetics has not been warmly received (Heck, 1998).

Despite the mainstream resistance to these concerns, a complex aesthetics continues to promote art and modes of cognition that are: (1) capable of identifying ideological inscriptions in aesthetic criticism, the artistic canon and other cultural forms; and (2) able and willing to challenge them. In the context of the "Sensation" conflict the highly sophisticated and urbane art community was unable to argue the point to Mayor Giuliani and other advocates of censorship that an important aspect of artistic production in a democratic society involves social, cultural and political critique. Few in the art world could articulate the importance of protecting the work of artists whose perspectives on the social order contribute to our cognitive, political, ethical and aesthetic development.

Some individuals did argue for artistic freedom from censorship—obviously an extremely important issue. But in this particular situation, such an argument did not address the variety of issues raised by the reactions to "Sensation." What was at stake was the cognitive and political role of art in confronting and changing human consciousness (Becker, 2000). As art breaks through parameters of expectation and reveals new ways of seeing and thinking, it performs a unique and valuable role in a democratic society. Once this process is closed off and limited to only what is "acceptable" to particular forms of dominant power, another thread is removed from the democratic tapestry; another perspective is erased from our multiple ways of seeing. The human state of being is reduced.

A Complex Aesthetics and Social Action: From the Cognitive into the Political

Art is dangerous—unregulated, it is subversive to the status quo. It tends to confront thoughtlessness and expose ignorance. When art is banished from the curriculum as a frill or censored because of its insult to "the things we hold dear," we lose a valuable agent of moral, social, cognitive, political and educational change. The cognitive change initiated by art in a complex aesthetics is an initial step in a larger process of sociopolitical action. In our concept of a complex aesthetics we cannot simply be spectators in the cultural and artistic realms who sit back and let the world come to us. We must gain the ability—art educators must teach the ability—to translate our aesthetically generated artistic, social, political, cultural, psychological and educational knowledge into ethical action.

The point is that as we connect the cognitive to the political in the context of a complex aesthetics, we engage in personal growth and sociopolitical change. As a teacher and a scholar interested in the cultural realm in relation to the political, cognitive and educational domains, I am fascinated with art's ability to transmit alternative views of the world and self, values and ethical insights. A complex aesthetic carefully attends to the specifics of this process and uses the sensitivities gained in its larger project. Such sensitivities and their cultivation rest at the heart of a democratic politics, higher-order thinking and a rigorous progressive education. With them we can better trace the forces that have shaped our consciousness and in the process become both more self-directed and connected to our peers.

Indeed, a complex aesthetics is interested in the way art connects us to the world. It rejects an art that removes us from interaction with the world and sequesters us in the elitist shelter of high art and elite culture with all the condescension toward the unwashed that this entails. As we are connected to the world in a complex aesthetics, we gain the opportunity to raise questions about those perspectives that are "certified"—a cognitive and political act that is prerequisite to social action. Like many before us, including members of traditional African cultures, we believe that works of art are much more than pictures, sculptures and other *objects*—they possess a special power, if not magical then at least sacred, that can not only connect us to the world and each other but produce a better, smarter, more progressive society (Dunn, 1998; Heck, 1998; Beyer, 2000; Greene, 1988; Jordan and Weedon, 1995).

Thus, we cannot separate the transformation of consciousness from the political domain. In much of my previous work I have referred to the effort to politicize cognition, that is, to expose the fact that the way we describe and act on our understanding of cognition always has political consequences (Kincheloe and Steinberg, 1993; Kincheloe, Steinberg and Villaverde, 1999; Kincheloe, Steinberg and Tippins, 1999). Thus, the way art enhances our cognitive ability is a political function—though it is rarely recognized as such. When art challenges the modernist hyperrationalism and the positivist epistemology that supports it, it is directly challenging existing power relations in the United States in the first decade of the twenty-first century. Without such challenges, public conversation ceases; the political realm atrophies—as it already has in this society (Heck, 1998).

In this book, Karel Rose implores us to take advantage of the ability of aesthetics "to open new vistas, blur traditional boundaries and reach out to new definitions." The critical aesthetics referenced here requires intercultural conversations in art as a catalyst for Rose's vision. As we have explored the connections between art, culture, politics, cognition and education, we used racial examples involving the whiteness of the Western art establishment vis-à-vis the nonwhite outsiders both within the United States and other Western societies and African, Asian and indigenous artists. One of the quickest and most important ways to open new vistas, blur traditional boundaries and reach out to new definitions, I contend, involves social action that institutes full racial and ethnic participation in the various dimensions of artistic work.

In addition to the intrinsic justice of such social action the power of difference and the consciousness it creates would benefit everyone. Race, racism, ethnicity and ethnic bias would no longer be viewed as problems of so-called people of color but the responsibility of everyone. Focusing on anti-racism and anti-ethnic bias, a critical aesthetics would make art a primary force in the quest for just multicultural societies. Like other cultural institutions in the United States, the art establishment has had great difficulty coming to terms with the nation's changing racial composition. We could clearly see this dynamic at work at the Brooklyn Museum, as the "Sensation" controversy began to unfold. How much better informed we are to read "Sensation" after grappling with the questions raised in the various chapters here. How much better equipped we are to recognize the multiple dimensions of the power of art in the cultural, political, cognitive and educational domains. In this context art realizes its potential as it steps boldly into the social arena.

References

Adler, S. (1991). Forming a critical pedagogy in the social studies methods class: The use of imaginative literature. In B. Tabachnick & K. Zeichner (Eds.), *Issues and practices in inquiry-oriented teacher education*. New York: Falmer.

Allen, G. (1995). Cultural studies in the undergraduate program: Pedagogical renaissance or curriculum life? <http://www.towson.edu/~sallen/CLST/lecture.html>.

Becker, C. (2000). The Brooklyn Museum. <http://humanities;uchicago/edu/artspublic/conf2000/becker.html>.

Benshoff, H. (1999). Heigh-ho, is Disney high or low? From silly cartoons to postmodern politics? <http://www.chapman.edu/animation/harryb.html>.

Best, S., & Kellner, D. (1991). *Postmodern theory: Critical interrogations*. New York: Guilford.

Beyer, L. (2000). *The arts, popular culture, and social change*. New York: Peter Lang.

Bohm, D., & Peat, F. (1987). *Science, order, and creativity*. New York: Bantam.

Borgmann, A. (1992). *Crossing the postmodern divide*. Chicago: University of Chicago Press.

Briggs, J., & Peat, F. (1989). *Turbulent mirror*. New York: Harper and Row.
Bronner, S. (1988). Between art and utopia: Reconsidering the aesthetic theory of Herbert Marcuse. In R. Pippin, A. Feenberg, and C. Webel (Eds.), *Marcuse: Critical theory and the promise of utopia*. Westport, Connecticut: Bergin and Garvey.
Brown, N., & Szeman, I. (2000). *Pierre Bourdieu: Fieldwork in culture*. Lanham, Maryland: Rowman and Littlefield.
Brown, R. (1995). Realism and power in aesthetic representation. In R. Brown (Ed.), *Postmodern representations: Truth, power, and mimesis in the human sciences and public culture*. Urbana: University of Illinois Press.
Calinescu, M. (1987). *Five faces of modernity: Modernism, avant-garde, decadence, kitsch, postmodernism*. Durham, North Carolina: Duke University Press.
Cary, R. (1998). *Critical art pedagogy: Foundations for postmodern art education*. New York: Garland.
Cosentino, D. (2000). Hip-hop assemblage: The Chris Ofili affair. *African Arts, 33* (1), 40–51.
Cowen, T. (1999). In praise of commercial culture. <http://www.gmu.edu/departments/economics/Tyler/Chapter 1.htm>.
Denzin, N., & Lincoln, Y. (2000). *Handbook of qualitative research* (2nd ed.). Thousand Oaks, California: Sage.
Dobrin, R. (1987). The nature of causality and reality: A reconciliation of the ideas of Einstein and Bohr in the light of Eastern thought. In D. Ryan (Ed.), *Einstein and the humanities*. New York: Greenwood Press.
Dunn, A. (1998). Who needs a sociology of the aesthetic? Freedom and value in Pierre Bourdieu's rules of art? *Boundry, 2* (25), 1.
Gergen, K. (1991). *The saturated self: Dilemmas of identity in contemporary life*. New York: Basic Books.
Greene, M. (1988). *The dialectic of freedom*. New York: Teachers College Press.
Greene, M. (1995). *Releasing the imagination: Essays on education, the arts, and social change*. San Francisco: Jossey-Bass.
Gresson, A. (1995). *The recovery of race in America*. Minneapolis: University of Minnesota Press.
Gresson, A. (2002). *America's atonement*. New York: Peter Lang.
Hebdige, D. (1989). *Hiding in the light*. New York: Routledge.
Heck, M. (1998). Art making and aesthetic inquiry: Critical connections among centering, social transformation, and pedagogy. *Journal of Critical Pedagogy*, 2, 1.
Jordan, G., & Weedon, C. (1995). *Cultural politics: Class, gender, race and the postmodern world*. Cambridge, Massachusetts: Blackwell.
Kester, G. (1997). Learning from aesthetics: Old masters and new lessons. *Art Journal, 56*, 1.
Kincheloe, J. (1993). *Toward a critical politics of teacher thinking: Mapping the postmodern*. Westport, Connecticut: Bergin and Garvey.
Kincheloe, J. (2002). *The sign of the burger: McDonald's and the culture of power.* Philadelphia: Temple University Press.
Kincheloe, J., & McLaren, P. (2000). Rethinking critical theory and qualitative research. In N. Denzin and Y. Lincoln (Eds.), *Handbook of qualitative research* (2nd ed.). Thousand Oaks, California: Sage Publications.
Kincheloe, J., & Steinberg, S. (1993). A tentative description of post-formal thinking: The critical confrontation with cognitive theory. *Harvard Educational Review, 63* (3), 296–320.

Kincheloe, J., & Steinberg, S. (1997). *Changing multiculturalism*. London: Open University Press.

Kincheloe, J., Steinberg, S., & Hinchey, P. (1999). *The post-formal reader: Cognition and education*. New York: Falmer Press.

Kincheloe, J., Steinberg, S., Rodriguez, N., & Chennault, R. (1998). *White reign: Deploying whiteness in America*. New York: St. Martin's Press.

Kincheloe, J., Steinberg, S., & Tippins, D. (1999). *The stigma of genius: Einstein, consciousness, and education*. New York: Peter Lang.

Kincheloe, J., Steinberg, S., & Villaverde, L. (Eds.). (1999). *Rethinking intelligence: Confronting psychological assumptions about teaching and learning*. New York: Routledge.

Lincoln, Y., & Guba, E. (1985). *Naturalistic inquiry*. Beverly Hills, California: Sage.

Mandell, S. (1987). A search for form: Einstein and the poetry of Louis Zukofsky and William Carlos Williams. In D. Ryan (Ed.), *Einstein and the humanities*. Westport, Connecticut: Greenwood.

Marcuse, H. (1955). *Eros and civilization*. Boston: Beacon.

O'Sullivan, E. (1999). *Transformative learning: Educational vision for the twenty-first century*. New York: Zed.

Padgham, R. (1988). Correspondences: Contemporary curriculum theory and twentieth-century art. In W. Pinar (Ed.), *Contemporary curriculum discourses*. Scottsdale, Arizona: Gorsuch Scarisbrick.

Percy, M. (1999). The visual unconsciousness: Contemporary allegories of seeing. <http://humanities.uchicago.edu/humanities/maph/percy.html>.

Rodriguez, N., & Villaverde, L. (1999). *Dismantling white privilege*. New York: Peter Lang.

Rorschach, K. (2000). The Brooklyn Museum controversy and the art museum paradigm. <http://humanities.uchicago.edu/artspublic/conf2000/rorschach.html>.

Ruesga, G. (1996). Singing and dancing in a baser manner: A plea for the democratization of taste. *Journal of Popular Culture, 29*, 4.

Slaughter, R. (1989). Cultural reconstruction in the post-modern world. *Journal of Curriculum Studies, 3*, 255–270.

Smart, B. (1992). *Modern conditions, postmodern controversies*. New York: Routledge.

Sorrentino, G. (1997). Writing for their lives. <http://daily.stanford.org/intermission/6-4-97/features/intsorrentino04.html>.

Stossel, S. (1998). The much publicized intellectual conflicts of the last decade. <http://www2.theatlantic.com/unbound/graffiti/ag9809.htm>.

Talbot, M. (1986). *Beyond the quantum*. New York: Bantam Books.

Talbot, M. (1991). *The holographic universe*. New York: HarperCollins.

Turner, F. (1996). The birth of natural classicism. *The Wilson Quarterly, 20*, 1.

Walsh, D. (1999). Some issues raised by the Brooklyn Museum exhibit. <http://www.wsws.org/articles/1999>.

Welch, S. (1991). An ethic of solidarity and difference. In H. Giroux (Ed.), *Postmodernism, feminism, and cultural politics: Redrawing educational boundaries*. Albany, New York: State University of New York Press.

Wilson, S. (1993). Light and dark visions: The relationship of cultural theory to art that uses emerging technologies. <http://mercury.sfsu.edu/~swilson/papers/postmodernism.pap.html>.

FOUR

"Sensation" at Brooklyn College: The Nation Responds

Karel Rose

An exhibit of eighty-six paintings, sculptures, multimedia installations and photographs by forty-one artists from the Saatchi Collection—"Sensation"—was shown at the Brooklyn Museum of Art from October 2, 1999, through January 9, 2000. In the museum's flyer, there was a warning that the exhibit contained material that some visitors might find objectionable. And indeed, they did. The exhibit resonated because of its open confrontation with issues surrounding gender, class, religion, race, normalcy, eccentricity, violence, disease and death. According to some viewers and to some who didn't even visit the museum, this exhibit was an outrage. People were forced to confront some deep feelings about notions of beauty, beliefs about the nature of art and personal beliefs systems about right and wrong, good and bad. The show and the public response so clearly raised questions about fantasy and reality, horror and humor, acceptance and rejection, sensation and reality that went beyond the museum walls that I began to remember my own childhood responses to authority, exclusion and the limitations imposed by my appointed life.

I suspect that everyone thinks the voices of their own childhood are like everyone else's. The hidden curriculum at my elementary school was as rigidly prescribed as the Early Bird Special. Each day I would place my clean handkerchief on the desk, show my nails for inspection and on Fridays show up in the required assembly uniform, a white blouse, red tie and navy blue skirt. There were clear rules about what was "right." In this world of absolutes, there was the right way to speak (perfect English grammar), the right place to live (in a one-family detached house), the right clothes to wear (pastels and white gloves) and the right food to order at Schraffts, the local upscale restaurant (watercress tea sandwiches). Race, ethnicity, class, gender and religion were inscribed in these prescriptions. If there were multiple voices on these issues, I never heard them. For this public elementary school in Brooklyn had a private agenda and packed my suitcase only with those cloaks woven in their smug establishment. Even prior to entering school, my suitcase was stuffed with metaphorical clothes spun from the cloth of "shoulds" and "oughts" by my parents, my religion, my neighborhood, my grandparents, the kids in my sandbox, Uncle Don and the ladies in my mother's Tuesday night Mah Jong game. Like many others, I was not allowed to explore or even look upon the "delicious" forbidden. I didn't know until I was an adult that I had permission to open the suitcase, take out the clothes, hold them up to the sunlight, to see if they still fit, and more significantly, decide if I liked them. I had not yet been emboldened by feminists like Julia Kristeva and Adrianne Rich and did not know that I could question their appropriateness for my life or more importantly that the major task of life might be to find one's life. At ten years old, I couldn't know that I was on a metaphysical quest, but that's when it all began. It wasn't until I was old enough to take the trolley car to the Linden Boulevard Library, read deeply and go to museums and theaters did I understand that there were a wide range of voices out there that could help me unpack my suitcase. Aesthetic experiences would be my road not taken. This awareness evolved into one of my reasons for becoming a teacher. Education is all about falling in love with knowing, asking questions and empowering people to think for themselves. We begin to learn when confronted with questions that are irksome, challenging and downright scary.

The next section describes a course that presented both students and instructors with alarming personal and cultural issues. The connections among philosophy, art and teaching become apparent when teachers encourage individual expression as a means of uncovering meaning. The work of philosopher Suzanne Langer grounds my thinking. Both the teacher and the artist create new forms. In their own ways, Georgia O'Keeffe transforms the reality of a poppy, Mark Morris re-visions classical themes into contemporary dances and Maya Angelou in *I Know Why the Caged Bird Sings* alters perceptions about early school experiences. Each re-codes and re-invents his or her world. Similarly, the artful teacher works with the curriculum, encoding it with expressive intention. Langer tells us, and it is helpful to think of teaching from this perspective, that every work of art is an objectification of subjective life (1956, p. 9). John Dewey's insights about the necessary relationship among culture, art and education and James Olney's (1972) metaphors of self helped me to better understand how our personal suitcases are packed with the commands of our cultures.

The Brooklyn College Experience

Brooklyn College is located in New York City, a cultural and artistic capital. A superabundance of live resources attracts our students. There are blockbuster museum exhibits, pop concerts, Shakespeare in the Park, opera, dance, poetry readings and theatre in every borough of the city. There is also an outrageous street life which is its own art form. Festivals, fairs, parades, markets, music and mime transform the city into a multicultural stage set. Our students are exposed to a sensual feast of images, sights, sounds and smells and a rare opportunity to engage with unmediated messages even as they walk from the subway to the college. A synesthesia takes hold when students give themselves permission to reflect on the voluptuous world that surrounds them. We encourage students to appropriate this artful world both as producers and consumers and recognize that museums and concert halls are public places, not private sanctuaries for a privileged few.

The Scholars Program at Brooklyn College invites instructors to develop challenging interdisciplinary courses that breathe new energy into old themes. The courses are meant to be dislocating and exotic. They ask the professors and students to challenge conventional pedagogy and curriculum. Joe Kincheloe and I wanted to work with undergraduates and conflate frequently segmented aspects of curriculum by viewing culture through the lens of art. Art experiences have the potential for removing the safety net of our own experiences. We wanted our students to question the context and discourse under which we were operating. Why these texts? Why these art works? Why these museums? The epistemological questions were to be theirs as they explored the belief systems of the storytellers of the culture, the artists and teachers. Joe and I talked, e-mailed and argued but finally developed the scaffolding for a course that we hoped would assist students to confront the relationships among art, culture and education. We asked impossible questions: What is beauty? What is culture? Can art be judged and if so how? What is the connection between truth and beauty? How are art and propaganda related?

We also needed to acknowledge the integrity of art for art's sake while recognizing how the art form itself disciplines the artist. Art is not simply an aesthetic doughnut from which you squeeze the jelly of personal meaning. Artists prepare their creations controlled by their passions, the subject matter and the medium. But a work of art is ironic; the artist takes some distance and creates a world with a different kind of reality. This ironic tone permits the viewer to see over the head of the situation and say "Yes, that is a true feeling. I know because I have felt that way." Similarly, we want our students through engagements with art to reconsider the beliefs that they have long accepted.

The artist through distance or point of view is positioned to assist the hospitable participant in this endeavor. When Robert Frost tells us in his poem that "good fences make good neighbors," his tone is ironic and asks us to scale metaphorical walls. In a different way, Andy Warhol's presentation of the mundane Campbell's soup can asks the viewer to question her preconception of the object. Encounters with art are a way, though by no means the only way, of providing students with the personal agency and safety to question the meaning of meaning.

On the Road from "High Art" and "Low Art" to "Sensation"

The proposed course for the Scholars Program invited students to unpack their bulging suitcases, examine and consider replacing some of the clothes, with the understanding that even the new garments might last for only a short time. They agreed. What we had going for us was a motivated and inquiry hungry group, the rich, ethnically diverse resources of New York City, and our faith in the arts as a vehicle for students to confront their own thoughts. The seminar was structured as an ongoing conversation about the ways in which art, culture and the self are entangled. We would study the slippery art of propaganda which appropriates beauty for its own ends. Our catchy title, "High and Low Art: Good and Bad Taste," was designed to seduce students into a consideration of how traditions and insights about the arts develop. They would be invited into the aesthetic gymnasium of popular and contemporary culture and asked to consider the power of slogans and labels. Does the assumption of "high" immediately suggest that lurking somewhere in the underbelly was "low"? Does it have to be either/or? Who decides? Here is the student flyer:

> *Rent* and *La Boheme* are stories about love affairs in which people sing and dance their angst and joys on stage. *La Boheme* may be performed at the Metropolitan Opera House, *Rent* in an Off-Broadway theatre. One story belongs to popular culture; the other as opera is termed "high art." Have you ever wondered why a Norman Rockwell illustration has been considered of less worth, financially and

> artistically, than a Picasso painting? Is there "bad" music and "good" dance? How do you differentiate between so-called "high" and "low" art? Who decides? The course will explore the cultural, racial, class and gender assumptions that underlie these categories and distinctions. Since New York City is an ideal milieu for encountering diversity in the arts, visits, and live performances in addition to a variety materials will serve as our texts.

Twelve students signed up for the course. Joe and I were counting on their extraordinary and diverse backgrounds combined with the resources of the city and a wide range of readings to help us integrate frequently segmented aspects of the college curriculum. To our surprise, a Goldilocks moment happened...a bowl of porridge, a chair and a bed that were "just right" figuratively flew into our classroom. The "Sensation" exhibit from London opened at the Brooklyn Museum of Art. It would be difficult to gainsay the teachable moment or the home-grown fusion and confusion that erupted when high and low culture met without an appointment. We were all wired for learning.

The "Sensation" exhibit was a high profile event, and the press and TV coverage that extolled its sensationalism certainly got the attention of our undergraduates. One painting, Chris Ofili's "Holy Virgin Mary" caused the most intense response. It was a large semi-abstract collage of a black Virgin resting on two balls of resin-covered dung with cutouts of female body parts affixed with dung. Ofili, himself a Roman Catholic, and his defenders have explained why the painting is not meant to be offensive. Dung is frequently incorporated into African art and viewed as a fertility symbol; elephants represent power. The painting is rooted in African folk art and plays with assumptions about black culture. Time, place and who is looking seem to be at least part of the issue. Stephen Jay Gould in *Finders, Keepers* describes how collectors in the seventeenth and eighteenth centuries kept cabinets of human parts, heads, full bodies of babies, religious relics and other macabre specimens as a hobby. Natalie Angier (1998) tells us that "The capacity for shock is alive and well, and it is not confined to Brooklyn. It is ancient and new, universal and intimate."

"Sensation" caused an explosion. Art and politics collided, and the city became a cultural battleground which resulted in the mayor's attempt to withdraw funding from the museum, a judge's ruling on First Amendment rights and daily protests by religious groups in front of the museum requiring a police presence. Some art makes people nervous. It would be interesting to explore why an admittedly violent film like *Hannibal* which shows the eating of human brains and Eminem's sadistic lyrics about the killing of his mother are both tolerated and applauded even by those who revile a single painting and threaten censorship. What raw cultural nerve had been exposed? "Sensation" was discussed in every major magazine and newspaper in the country as well as in the international press. The ripple effect was felt throughout the art world. The culture war was more significant than the exhibit. Ironically, everyone involved profited from the publicity generated by "Sensation." You had to be under a rock not to know about the elephant dung, the formaldehyde-encrusted animals, the sliced pig and the surreal human bodies. There were multiple interpretations, and as the furor skyrocketed so did attendance at the Brooklyn Museum of Art.

The "Sensation" exhibit was a *deus ex machina* sent down to two earthling professors and their students for analyzing some of the most disturbing ideological questions of our time. John Dewey speaks about reflection and surrender in the learning process. This was the surrender part. Our experience may serve to assist other instructors when they are dealt an unexpected hand, a Goldilocks moment and the opportunity to re-think the delivery and content of their courses. In new ways, the concept of race and the crisis around white identity connected to questions about the canonization and intersection of western art with world cultures. From a different perspective, I am reminded of the destruction of religious statues by the Taliban in Afghanistan. The political and social issues of our time were inscribed in this exhibit and suggested paradigms for many action research projects. The issues were apparent and the evidence so omnipresent that students could work as archaeologists with only a feather for brushing away the dust from their artifacts. We were overtaken by questions about culture, totalitarianism, feminism, religion and racism which were just waiting to be studied. We continued to focus attention on our original concerns about prevailing values and extant epistemology, but the context had changed. The epithets "degenerate," "anti-American," "sick," "corrupting," "unnatural," "subversive" highlighted the ambiguous and passionate responses that this exhibit evoked.

There were multiple questions for students to research. What should be in a museum? What is art? What is beauty? Is the art world out of touch? What happens when power and art collide? Do the arts have to be made bulletproof? Can aesthetic quality be separated from ideology? If there were any answers, they were elusive. The case was still in the courts and our students became a self-appointed jury of scholars. A new course outline gave birth to itself fortified by resources in the form of legal briefs, scholarly discussions in journals and daily articles in the national press.

This mini-event, an exhibition in Brooklyn, had caused a tidal wave of responses from philosophers, politicians, art historians, psychologists, accountants, lawyers, religious leaders and social critics. Not since the Brooklyn Dodgers won the World Series in 1955 had Brooklyn been so visible. Suddenly around the country people were claiming only "six degrees of separation" from Brooklyn, their birth mother.

The New Course

We shared with the students the inappropriateness of continuing business as usual, and they agreed that the transformation of the course was the course. We would be a work in progress, a studio for the exploration of process and product. As the instructors, we were forced to re-think the intersections between curriculum and pedagogical practices within the larger Deweyian frame of social consciousness. "Sensation" would serve as the resource, and both students and instructors would create a study guide for the projects. We were becoming a community of scholars. The disciplines of history, economics, education, art, women's studies, sociology, and so forth, and the themes of censorship, private interests, the media, religion, power, public funding for the arts and the upcoming presidential election would be used as the lens but would not be discrete entities. There would be an uncontrollable fallout as students crossed their own borders and recognized the relationships between art and economics, history and women's studies, education and sociology. "Sensation," the course and the exhibit was an unusual opportunity to explore how taken-for-granted assumptions surface when art, culture and politics intersect. Paulo Freire's ideas about critical literacy came to life. The students began to see beyond the limited situations imposed by their own backgrounds and identify the generative themes which moved their inquiry beyond the borough of Brooklyn.

As students posed problems, the principles of John Dewey emerged, connecting reflection, action and democracy. Students were not only showing up for every class but wide awake, impelled by their need to know. Their insights and findings were fresh, impassioned and rich. They enlightened all of us as they courageously took out and then returned some of the clothes to their suitcases. They also shared their research in a public forum for the whole college. We are very proud of their work, which reflects an appreciation of the seamlessness of knowledge and the influence of culture on meaning making. The titles of their final papers provide clues to the depth and breadth of their insights: "Cultural Literacy and Art," "British Beginnings of the 'Sensation' Exhibit," "Morality, Culture and 'Sensation,'" "The Mayor, the Museum and the Masses," "Power and Politics," "Art, Education and Its Effects," "The General Will and Art," "The Function of a Museum," "Art for Freedom," "The Naked and the Nude," "Religious Meaning and 'Sensation.'" It should be noted that not all the students were creative or competent writers. However, impelled by their connection to their chosen topic, every student submitted a meaningful, well-written document.

The "Sensation" Forum

On December 2, 1999, the Ethyle R. Wolfe Institute for the Humanities at Brooklyn College in cooperation with the School of Education sponsored a six-hour forum where these remarkable undergraduates presented their eclectic papers. They worked the day before the presentation putting up posters, photographs, cartoons and their own art work. They distributed questionnaires, bibliographies, surveys and their own papers. All their work testified to a personal engagement with the material but also highlighted a pedagogical sophistication unusual even in graduate students. They further demonstrated an ability to present a very controversial personal and public issue to a divided audience. The students were by no means of one mind about religion, culture or art. Aside from brief introductions, both Joe and I took a backseat. By this time, the students owned the forum and the course. Here are some excerpts from their presentations:

> As a child, I've often heard the term "cultured" used in adult conversations. I never knew exactly what the word meant but I associated it with operas, ballets and museums, places that require somewhat formal attire. As an adult student, I can now look back upon my student-child experiences and notice the seemingly innocuous way in which I was trained to view art, trained to appreciate the works of art my teachers revered, trained to conform my aesthetic taste to the ideal American aesthetic standard. It was only very recently that I re-trained myself to no longer believe that "culture" needed to conform to the *Merriam Webster Dictionary* definition: "refinement of intellectual and artistic taste." Ironically, my re-training and changed belief occurred when I enrolled myself in a special honors course that I believed would help me in my pursuit to become "cultured."
>
> —Maggie Mosseri

> More than two hundred years ago, King George III founded the Royal Academy of Art in Piccadilly, which is in central London. The Academy gathered a reputation for being too stuffy and regal over those years. Until the mid-1990s, it had

been more than two million pounds in debt because its attendance levels had dwindled significantly. The British public had lost interest in the museum, and they thought of it as a palace of dust. It had a deficit of about 715,000 pounds. Unlike the Brooklyn Museum of Art, it receives no public subsidies. Then in the summer of 1997, the Academy's Exhibitions' Secretary, Norman Rosenthal decided to mount a show titled, "Sensation: Young British Artists of the Saatchi Collection." The exhibit opened to record crowds on September 18, 1997, and ran through December 28, 1997. In that short time, it managed to draw more than 300,000 visitors who paid up to seven pounds each for admission. The Academy was pulled out of their significant debt and appreciated the exhibition. But not everyone was happy. Several top officials in the Academy resigned because they objected to the material in "Sensation." Yet it was the objectionable material in the exhibit that had helped it to draw record crowds in its limited run. Most of the furor was caused by a single portrait, but it wasn't Chris Ofili's, "Holy Virgin Mary." It was "Myra," a portrait of a child molester and murderer.

—Elizabeth Paredes

I never knew that I "got" Picasso, Pollack and everyone else. The High Art/Low Art seminar from which this work was born, completely changed my idea of art. I am not saying that I had much of an idea about what art was before this course, but the few things that I always assumed as staples of the world were joyfully shattered. Prior to this seminar, my art experience was limited to the college's core art course, calligraphy in high school and some of my own poor attempts to make visual art. To me art was still to be seen in a series and judged by the standards of pretty, not pretty and wow, that piece is really old and done by someone really famous. In some ways I was opened up to an unshared dream; the purpose of going to see art was no longer to a touch a 300-year-old painting or a well-known sculpture when no one was looking so that I could say that I did. Free from the elite's curating hand, I saw that art is not objective; there is not really right, only an established one.

I could never write everything that I learned, but here is what comes to mind on Monday night, right after "Ally McBeal." I learned to question what art is, what is high or low art and who decides. I learned that art is not only for the elite. Western art by "dead white men" is not by definition necessarily the apex of all art. I learned that sometimes it's okay not to know or that there is no answer. I learned that I am an artist.

—Joseph Mantovani

Many students attended the forum. Their comments provide further insights about the larger questions surrounding art, culture and the definition of knowl-

> edge. I was extremely impressed with the fact that students were able to articulate a strong passion for art and recognize the political ramifications surrounding it. Since nowadays many students rarely voice a political opinion or even vote, this was very important to me.
>
> —Mark Trachtenberg

> Although I've always embraced all forms of art whether I found them aesthetically pleasing or not, the "Sensation" symposium was an eye opener. I think that I understand the magnitude of the controversy, but I cannot accept a mayor's control over art. Art is human expression and that in itself is beautiful. When art is made new, we are made new with it. Art gives human beings a connectedness to their own time and an understanding of the psychic energies that we share with others who engage with the work of art.
>
> —Brian Bell

> I believe that the mayor wants to be seen as a moral person because he is persecuting these artists. I believe that the artists are making a statement that we as a culture have to re-examine our morals. These artists, I believe, are lashing out at society and saying wake up and look what you are doing. I really believe that the mayor himself is afraid and doesn't want to see the ugly truth.
>
> — Jaclyn Collins

A film by Roy Doremus, *Sensation: People Speak Out*, was shown at the forum. Aired on television several times during the exhibition, it documented the opening days of "Sensation." Mr. Doremus, who lives across the street from the Brooklyn Museum of Art, spoke to the group and recounted his conversations with the people from France, Mexico, Israel and Japan (many art critics among them) who had come to view the exhibit. In my interview with Mr. Doremus, a visual artist as well as a film maker, he explained how his personal experiences had influenced his work. "A lot of my art confronts issues of power and manipulation," he said. I asked what he thought should not be in a museum. Thinking for a while he said, "Anything shallow, contrived, superficial, superficial, thoughtless." In discussing what might be considered obscene, his response was narrowness and blindness to others' perspectives. He provided this anecdote to illustrate his concern about the results of forced limitations. "I catch mice in a live trap, so I can then set them free in an appropriate place. I've found, however, that after the mouse is in the cage for more than a day, it is reluctant to leave. We, like the mice," he concluded, "must have an enormous need to be boxed in with the many others who are confined." I was reminded of Susan Sontag's comment that every reductive tendency stems from terror.

At the forum, Katha Politt, a columnist well known for her sharp and provocative analyses of popular culture and politics in *The Nation*, acknowledged that before seeing the "Sensation" show, she was prepared "to come away with gloomy thoughts." However, there were some works of art that she found both interesting and beautiful. Even so, yes, she also found some of the art repellent. Nevertheless, her real concerns seemed to supercede the specifics of the art itself. They are worthy of notice. She says:

> Teenagers, not usually caught dead in museums, are going. . . . Aesthetic and political conservatives have been complaining about modern art ever since there was any. . . . The history of this critique should give us pause—more often [it's led to] bonfires than to artworks of lasting interest. (Polit 1999, p. 10)

Mark Green, public advocate to the City of New York, shared his friend of the court brief, outlining his concern about the mayor's threat to withdraw the museum's city funding. Jane Miller-Kerina, author and lecturer in the Africana Studies Department at Brooklyn College, enlightened the group with background on African art forms. She was followed by Dread Scott (see the appendix for the text of Scott's remarks).

So What?

In a previous chapter, Joe asked, "Says Who?" I would now like to ask, "So What?" This chapter has discussed the connections among art, philosophy, education and culture, recognizing that as each discipline searches for meaning, it creates carefully reasoned arguments to support its existence. But since all thinking cannot be reduced to logic, we want to encourage our readers to plant knowledge in the ground of human experience. The "Sensation" exhibit granted the two of us this opportunity by providing the ultimate teachable moment. Reaching out to the students in our class and in the community, we have included student responses, artist reactions and the comments of people whose interests are generated by their politics and cultural commitments. Though the relationships among art, philosophy, education and culture are not always explicit, each discipline "does" philosophy in its search for meaning. Philosophical inquiry undergirds the work of the artist, the teacher and the culturalist. Suzanne Langer tells us, "There is nothing one cannot philosophize about—that is, there is nothing that does not offer some philosophical problems" (1956, p. 9). From this perspective, we are all predestined to inquire, to ask but not necessarily answer questions about the human condition in which we find ourselves. Very often, it is the status quo that comes under inquiry. How personally difficult it is to be out of step with our times. However, it is the artist who may provide us with a "safe remove" as we privately contemplate another's interpretation of the world, or a teacher may hold our hand as we walk down a gravelly road. A cry of pain from an eloquently rendered work of art can provide us with courage. Notwithstanding, meekness overcomes me when I consider the hostility that can result from our questions. "What right do we have to question the wisdom and logic of the ages?" Not all of us can or should be Socrates, prepared to die for the truth. And is it possible that dying for the "truth" may not be good for the world?

This chapter is designed to focus on questions not answers. Trust the process and you will find yourselves thinking like an aesthetician and ask what is art? Or a philosopher and ask what is truth? Or an educator and ask what does it mean to teach someone something? Or a culturalist and ask how does the sociocultural matrix alter perception, thinking and behavior? Each of these questions is inter-related. Joe Kincheloe, Patrick Slattery and Shirley Steinberg in *Contextualizing Teaching* (2000) speak to the imperative of contextualizing rather than fragmenting our search for the answers to these questions but always grounding our responses in human experience.

There will be many "Sensations" as we run the course in our teaching lives. Be consoled that you are not alone in confronting the new, the disparate, the heretic and revolting aspects of life. Your good judgment, your open-mindedness, your creative willingness and your courage to confront revulsion, contradiction and ambiguity will help you to place your own life's work in perspective. Just as there are no cures for certain diseases, no assurances about what is around the corner, there are no answers to certain questions. *So What?!*

References

Angier, N. (1999, October 5). The shock of the natural. *The New York Times*, pp. E1, 2.

Gould, Stephen J. (1993) *Finders keepers*. New York: Random House.

Kincheloe, J., Slattery, P., & Steinberg, S. (2000). *Contextualizing teaching*. New York: Longman.

Langer, S. (1956). *Problems of art*. New York: Scribners.

Olney, James (1972). *Metaphors of self: The meaning of autobiography*. Princeton, NJ: Princeton University Press.

Politt, K. (1999, November 1). Catholic bashing. *The Nation*, p. 10.

FIVE

ARTS AND SOCIETY: ART, SCIENCE AND TEACHING

Karel Rose

Arts and Society is a graduate course offered by Lesley University in the Creative Arts in Education program at sites throughout the country. In this course, practicing teachers at different grade levels and disciplines have the opportunity to visit museums and attend music, dance and theater events. A non-objective painting, a surrealist poem, a pre-Columbian pot or a piece of rap music can elicit an "ah ha" response and deliver to the instructor the much awaited teachable moment. Artistic expressions are seductive, excite our sensibilities and make us think. Though everyone views art through the lens of personal experience and their own cognitive maps, it is useful to explore and articulate the foundations for these assumptions, schemata and tastes. Reflections on experience build bridges to new ways of acting in and on the world. Teachers and artists, as interpolators of culture, are in a powerful position to polish, refurbish and augment extant knowledge. In this sense, teaching is political. The interpolator, the students and the content are transformed. Bill Beckley, the art critic, reminds us that every aesthetic choice, as well, is political. Neither artists nor teachers engage in a neutral activity.

The Lesley University Experience

When I teach "Arts and Society," my deepest concern has been how to assist practicing educators to recognize their power to change the world albeit one student a time. I struggle with how the educational system might interrupt the processes that oppress people because of gender, race, class, ethnicity and/or age. Moral philosopher Jonathan Glover and the poet Robert Bly, each in their own way, express their deep concern about the patterns of cruelty humans have inflicted on each other throughout the course of history. Bly (2001) laments that "The greedy one in us will still survive." While Glover (1999) who documents the many instances of unrelieved callousness in the twentieth century from the Holocaust to the current atrocities of ethnic cleansing, makes a strong case for understanding our own inhumanity. Naturally, other voices find political and social circumstances central to understanding the continuing violations of human rights. UNESCO documents deny that violent behavior is genetically programmed into human nature. Clearly, whatever the answer, the question is how do we build support among the peoples of the world to avoid continuing moral disasters. As educators, we are in a position to build that support. Even if optimism is off the mark, we can do nothing else but emphasize the countervailing human responses of sympathy, empathy, personal and moral identity and self-respect as a human being. The work of philosopher Nel Noddings is rooted in this ethic of care. She asserts, "It is gratifying how often we can really see a better self if we look for one, and its identification is a first step in its realization" (1992). Noddings identifies and implores teachers to take notice of the many opportunities for caring that present themselves in their personal and professional lives.

It is with this perspective that I ask students in all my courses to think about a social issue that enrages them. Is it poverty? Child abuse? Rape? Racial discrimination? Censorship? After ten years of asking this question, I am no longer surprised that some students are unable to identify a single issue. I do not believe that this highlights a lack of social consciousness but rather that they are unable or unwilling to connect the private and public spheres of their lives to larger cultural forces. Locked into what Paulo Freire identifies as a limit situation, some are unaware of the larger generative themes in society that, in fact, do control their personal worlds. Many students do speak eloquently about their commitments and describe how they challenge the dominant discourse. I describe later on some of their poignant personal experiences and how their outsider status, their childhood and adolescent terrors, prepared them to assist others and make caring central in their lives. These stories have propelled me into developing strategies to access the wellsprings of these experiences, through the use of aesthetic experiences and autobiography. When personal experience is better understood, it may ultimately be transformed into teaching behaviors that bring to life Dewey's precepts that education is the fundamental method of social progress and reform.

Aesthetic experiences serve as the opening wedge. Students write very artful and personal narratives of educational experience. They read Jung Chang's memoir, *Wild Swans*, in which she describes the lives of three generations of oppressed women in twentieth-century China. They view Pamela Gien's dramatic portrayal in the *The Syringa Tree* of her ambivalent childhood in apartheid South Africa. We share paintings and posters that depict the ravages of war, read the poetry of children from the Terezin concentration camp, play the songs of Bertolt Brecht and Kurt Weill and view Francisco de Goya's drawings of oppression. Something happens when a cry of pain with its ironic distance enters consciousness.

Percy Bysshe Shelley called poets, "the unacknowledged legislators of the world." The artist can be a powerful and persuasive catalyst for both good and evil. Oppressive regimes have always recognized how the propaganda machine uses the arts as sly and stealthy assistants in their propaganda machine and have paid close attention to aesthetic zing politics through theatrical ceremonies, rallies and the identification of subversive art. Standardizing what is acceptable art effectively closes down thinking and increases dependence on others' definitions of knowledge. Classrooms are places to counteract this pattern and utilize the arts to assist students to declare their cognitive independence.

During the "Arts and Society" course, we visit museums, listen to music and read poetry to each other. Students are asked to identify how similar themes are expressed in different cultures and mediums. They study how artists respond to social issues and to each other's works noting poems about paintings (John Updike's "Two Hoppers"), music about myths (Jacques Offenbach's "Orpheus in the Underworld") and films created from biographies (*Pollack*). The purpose is twofold: an appreciation of different aesthetic forms as well as the ideological commitments of certain works of art. I am careful not to exploit a work of art to establish a code of action but also note the inextricable relationship that exists between thought and aesthetic expression. Participants are encouraged to recognize and value their own independent responses. Some say, "yes" that is a true feeling; "I know because I have felt that way." A "feeling fact" honors an individual's reality and suggests an identification with another whose dailiness may be very different from one's own but whose sensual life bears striking similarities. The arts set down the roots for empathy and enable us to establish classrooms that encourage a learning environment in a cocoon of caring.

Some students choose to do their in-depth exploration of a social issue in an extensive research paper rather than a performance project. However, everyone needs to acknowledge the genesis of his or her social concern in personal experience and to understand the phenomenalogical and relational aspects of his or her thinking. Most students choose to do a multimodality performance project. In addition to the presentation, students submit a reflective paper on the process: how they came to know and care about this issue, their feelings and thoughts about the presentation itself and the response of their colleagues.

In project after project, certain themes have emerged. It may be helpful for teachers interested in heightening awareness of inequities and reconstructing the discourse in their classes to note how many social issues coalesce in a performance project. Projects about power are very frequently connected to concerns about outsiderness. Here is one example: Janet, a teacher in Seattle, presented a multimedia theater piece to express the concept of power as played out in her home. She reconstructed the unequal relationships in her upper middle-class white family with an alcoholic mom. For her performance, Janet brought in a huge pink elephant, which she placed on the table in front of us. "The problem was as visible as this elephant but it was never discussed," she said. As an only child, Janet would hear her parents, in the next room, arguing, throwing things, slamming doors, but she was always excluded. She showed a videotape of a failed birthday celebration for her mother in a local restaurant. In some ways, both her mother and she were outsiders but in different ways. Janet's body language was illuminating; she sat back from the table while her mother spoke primarily to the waiters who were attentive to refilling her glass. It became apparent that Janet's pain was as much connected to her outsiderness from the family as well as her distress over the alcoholism. Janet, a teetotaler, has worked with AA for years helping families cope and is now taking her presentation into the high schools of Tacoma. Many of those watching the presentation commented on the impact of her work in their final evaluations. The artistic product, no matter how personal, provides a safe remove in its objectification of the subjective.

For the observer, the cry of pain aesthetically rendered can cultivate empathy and encourage a connectedness to others. In the development of these projects, students recognize how their abilities to transform personal experience into aesthetic forms unleash knowing at a new level. Decision making about the powers of the artistic way of knowing illuminates complex concepts about how meaning is made, absorbed and changed. A deeper understanding of pedagogy emerges when teachers glimpse the power of the arts to alter the landscape of the learning/teaching life.

Art, Beauty and the Classroom

Many teachers want their classrooms to be places of beauty. They argue that wonder, spontaneity, playfulness and creativity are not only signifiers of beauty but the cherished rights (rites) of childhood. To teach someone something is a beautiful human act. To see learning happen is to bear witness to beauty. But there is ample evidence both in the United States and around the world to document the lack of beauty in many children's lives: nine-year-old boys in Honduras fall asleep exhausted while stitching baseballs, eleven-year-old Turkish girls spend their days knotting rugs and young adolescents work full-time in cloisonné factories in China. In our own country, Jonathan Kozol (2000), Alex Kotlowitz (1991) and Mike Rose (1990) testify to the lack of beauty in many children's lives, recording the poverty, fear and humiliation that suffuses their daily existence. Notions of beauty are further distorted when the murdered JonBenet Ramsey, a six-year-old beauty queen, becomes an icon for other children and their families.

Here are some thoughts about beauty as related to life in classrooms:

1. Beauty is students and teaches sharing common goals.
2. Beauty is engaged, active, reflective students.
3. Beauty is teachers listening and children speaking.

Searching for beauty in the artfulness of the black experience in America, I once wrote a book which took its name, *A Gift of the Spirit* (1971), from W.E.B. Du Bois's *The Souls of Black Folk*. Du Bois so eloquently voiced the Negroes' gifts of story and song that I came to think of beauty and soul as almost synonymous. But because soulfulness may involve emotions of great pain, horror and anger, it seemed the more inclusive term. Beauty on the other hand is expected to delight and is usually associated with what is pleasing or attractive. Theodor Adorno, the German philosopher, writing after World War II, questioned whether it was even possible to aesthetically depict the Holocaust. He thought that it would be barbaric "to write poetry after Auschwitz." Yet we must grieve together about these atrocities and the process itself may be an aesthetic experience. I have seen artful memorials in the Great Synagogue in Budapest, the Diaspora Museum in Tel Aviv and in public squares in

Istanbul, Capetown and Pittsfield, Massachusetts, that are unforgettable and have shown me new ways to think about the Holocaust.

Can Negro spirituals be called beautiful despite the horrors they depict? What about the cries of anguish in the journals written by slaves stripped of their African traditions and sold into bondage? How can we think about Robert Capa's famous photographs of the Spanish Civil War or the poster of the victims of the My Lai Massacre? Must art be synonymous with beauty? We need a postmodern vocabulary which speaks of art as provocative, inclusive, empathic, contextual, accessible and relational. More likely art for today and tomorrow resides in everything which links us to one another. Beauty may be connectedness. That which links me to the human condition. Art experiences are not an exclusive, private, static, collusive activity reserved for a preselected group. The artistic and educational communities, both in their discourse and context, face the challenge of creating a climate that honors multiple voices and diverse ways of viewing the world. Our visual abilities help us to make sense of the world before our eyes but Donald Hoffman (1998), the cognitive scientist tells us that what we see is much more than our perceptual constructions.

Today, many artists do not see beauty and art as necessary partners. Louise Bourgeois, an internationally renowned sculptor, says beauty is something she never talks about (Beckley, 1998). In this book, Joe Kincheloe tells us that abstract expressionists like Jackson Pollack and Jasper Johns refused to "beautify" the world and their abstract works of art signify their resistance to fatuous representations of beauty. Is it a work of art if it does not depict a beautiful feeling or experience? Does it belong in a museum? How do you respond to Picasso's "Guernica," which depicts the horrors of war? Or to Frida Kahlo's self-portraits, which starkly portray her physical pain? ("I paint my own reality," she said.) Unwilling to get caught in the net of producing "beautiful" art, Edward and Nancy Reddin Kienholz use common artifacts from the everyday world, usually discarded furniture, to create constructions intended to make a cultural or political statements. Junk art and graffiti confuse us all the more when we try to place them within the boundaries of conventional definitions of beauty. Joe continues to ask us to rethink our notions of beauty as something always related to harmony and order. He suggests that in certain contexts beauty might be viewed as offensive. Art critics like the *New Yorker*'s Peter Schjedahl, note that there is a progressive divorce of beauty from art.

New ways of thinking about art and beauty have implications for the way we teach. If we only share with children the beautiful in the world, they will catch us in our game. It is dishonest to continue to speak in codes and euphemisms: "Grandpa's not dead; he passed away." The literal child will ask, "When will he pass by again?" Children know many truths. Third graders respond powerfully to *Sadako and the Thousand Paper Cranes*, Eleanor Coerr's award winning book about the devastation of Hiroshima. Similarly, Jacob Lawrence's picture book, *The Great Migration* created from his paintings of American slavery, raises horrific but very real questions about our moral obligations to each other. In 1998 and 1999, the Newbery Award, given for the best children's book of the year, went to Louise Sachar's *Holes* and to Christopher Curtis' *Bud, not Buddy*. Sachar's book, like many of her other works, is grim, depicting life in a juvenile detention facility. *Bud, not Buddy* is the story of a homeless boy during the Great Depression. The National Book Award for 2000 was given to Gloria Whelan's *Homeless Bird*, the story of a poor Indian girl who resists her traditional background and forges an exceptional future. These books are important because they acknowledge and elegantly document cries of pain about and for children.

From another perspective, what do we do with that myth of the beautiful Thanksgiving between the Indians and the Pilgrims? Tell the truth or make it pretty? In her work, the artist, Barbara Kruger critiques the disparity between the supposed beauty of visual advertising images and the reality of the message by placing bold banners across the image. In bold red-and-white letters the words "Whose values?" are superimposed on a *Newsweek* cover portrait altering and interrupting the intended message. Kruger implores us to question the idealized, nostalgic pictures and recognize how visual experiences deform our rational intelligence.

Using this more expansive template to think about beauty, consider how teachers in "Arts and Society" define notions of beauty in classrooms:

- Engagement is beautiful.
- Reflection is beautiful.
- Idiosyncratic ways of looking at the world are beautiful.
- Respectful connections to others are beautiful.
- Unlayering conflict and "getting to yes" are beautiful.
- Differences in culture, ethnicity, race, gender and class are beautiful.
- Building and honoring expressive capabilities are beautiful.
- Making meaning and knowing is beautiful.
- Teachers and students working together is beautiful.

Interpretations of beauty depend upon time, place, the classroom environment and the cultural surround of children's lives. Life in classrooms is all about one subjective, educational act after another, which transforms abstractions into actions through experience. For John Dewey, this perspective provides the medium through which thought and action mix. But teaching remains a multifaceted tapestry. The threads are both abstract and practical; they come from experience, emotions, logical thinking, the arts and the established canons. They cannot be packaged in separate parcels.

Teaching: A Science and an Art

Artists are temperamental, subjective, irrational and highly emotional. Scientists are rational, objective, abstract thinkers and highly intellectual. An artist is poor, lives in an unheated apartment and works through the night. He is supported by his current girlfriend or his family. A scientist works in a well-lit, meticulously clean laboratory surrounded by appreciative students, supported by funds from the corporate world. Many people want to marry a scientist; few people want to marry a poet, sculptor or dancer.

If you believe the above, you

1. don't know many artists or scientists
2. are watching too much mainstream television
3. are controlled by stereotypes

We all know temperamental, irrational scientists and cold-blooded, left-brained artists. Despite the prevailing mythology, research since the 1970s has shown that the arts not only address human sensibilities but are also intellectual disciplines of substance, powerfully connected to cognition. It is the "intuitive and imaginative powers (which) are the midwives to new forms of thought and conduct, new vistas and even new social institutions and systems" (Johnson, 1965 p. 2).

Science relies heavily on both intuition and imagination, and scientists testify to their own indebtedness to the aesthetic. Scientists, artists, plumbers, undertakers, nurses, teachers all create works that expand our ideas about what is beautiful. Albert Einstein on several occasions compared his way of working to that of painters and poets. Dancers, musicians and writers testify to the logic that gives birth to their artistry. Teaching, both an art and a science, requires that we fall from the safety of our discipline-based preconceptions in order to appreciate the multifaceted ways that knowing happens.

What follows are two experiences with teachers in the Lesley University Program which illustrate the complicated and symbiotic relationship between art and science.

> We are standing in front of a huge exhibit of a science laboratory at the Massachusetts Museum of Contemporary Art (MOCA) in North Adams, which, at first glance, appears to be a science laboratory, but a closer look reveals that something is awry. The familiar seems strange. The batteries draw power from flowers, salt and horseshoes. The markings on the lopsided, imperfectly shaped vessels say, "handfuls," "blunder," "boo-boo" and "matter of chance." Dice are scattered all over the lab table suggesting uncertainty. A major precept of science is that the experiments are objective. Yet in this science lab, everything is subjective, whimsical and poetic. Ee Andree Laramee has created an environment in which art critiques science. This "beautiful" installation is dislocating, for it blurs the lines between art and science, suggesting that subjectivity infuses all human activity.

> We move to another exhibit this time outside the building. It is titled "Tree Logic." In this installation, six live trees are inverted and suspended from a truss. Over time, these trees still grow towards the sun producing unusual, some might say, unnatural shapes. I am reminded of the beautiful baobab trees in Africa which are called "upside-down" trees because the roots appear to be growing from the top. Perfectly natural and logical for this tree say the teachers in a small school in Zimbabwe. How do we answer when a student asks "What is natural?" How do we explain what is logical? How do we distinguish appearance from reality? Who decides?

Here are two statements about ghetto conditions: the first by the social scientist, Kenneth B. Clark (1965), the second an excerpt from *Native Son*, a novel, by Richard Wright (1966).

> Poor housing conditions, malnutrition and inadequate health care are undoubtedly responsible for the high infant death rate, where flies and maggots breed where the plumbing is stopped up, and not repaired, where rats bite helpless infants; the conditions of life are brutal and inhuman. (p. 31)

> Buddy extended his hand. Bigger caught the skillet and lifted it high in the air. The rat scuttled across the floor and stopped again at the box and searched quickly for the hole; then it reared once more and bared long yellow fangs, piping shrilly, belly quivering. Bigger aimed and let the skillet fly with a heavy grunt. There was a shattering of wood as the box caved in. The woman screamed and hid her face in her hands. Bigger tiptoed forward and peered, "I got 'im," he muttered, his clenched teeth bared in a smile. "By God, I got 'im." (p. 10)

Both Clark and Wright have recorded their observations of slum experiences. Both excerpts have the ring of truth, but in each case it is a different order of truth. Wright's words are filled with feeling, so are Clark's. However, it is Wright's picture of reality that impresses me with a kind of universal truth about a feeling. Though slum life may not be common to all people, feelings of fear are universal. However, both the social scientist and the artist began their exploration of slum conditions because of an emotional response to the subject matter. Science and art seek answers in different ways. Neither discipline utilizes a purely factual approach for coming to know. Feeling facts and logic suffuse both disciplines for the form and process that science imposes on reality assist in the creation of knowledge. The point is the complementarity of both science and the arts while recognizing the subjectivity and limitations of singular ways of knowing.

There was a time when few would question the objectivity of science. Art, not science, was the safe haven for personal perspectives. However, as far back as 1897, John Dewey recognized the conjugal and dependent relationship between art and science as ways of knowing. "Science," he said, "is of value because it gives the ability the interpret and control the experience already had" ("My Pedagogic Creed").

Updating Dewey, here's how one class at Cornell Medical College is heightening observation skills through a visual arts course called, "The Art of Observation." The medical students view traditional paintings in the Frick Collection in New York City and are asked to carefully observe, contrast and compare visual clues of illness. Concerned that in an age of technology, medical imaging, skillful observations will be preempted by machines, these students are being asked to observe carefully the age of a subject in a portrait, or consider what the curvature of an arm might suggest. Learning how to see better, it is anticipated, will develop greater empathy and sympathy for teachers as well as physicians. Fortunately, Dewey is a wake-up call for many professionals who recognize that, whether working in the arts or sciences, we acquire knowledge through careful observation, engaging with symbols, challenging the familiar and experiencing the larger social context. In support of this perspective, Joe Kincheloe in this book states that "objective" judgments may have less to do with aesthetic or scientific concerns than with cultural values, class dynamic ideologies and even ethnic, racial and gender issues.

A leap of faith, a hypothesis, a reaching beyond the accepted parameters into the moment of discovery characterize both art and science. Neither the thinking nor the execution of either discipline proceeds in an orderly fashion. Teaching is much the same. It is never monotonic. Much like complex musical activity, it is drenched in the contrapuntal voices of logical and sensual thinking. How could it be otherwise?

Education, from the Latin *educere*, means to lead out, to open up to the world of ideas. These ideas originate in non-logical and non-verbal modes but then translate into symbolic languages. Teachers need not be ashamed to use words of feeling that honor their artistic and sensating selves when exploring all curriculum areas. Robert S. Root-Bernstein and Michele Root-Bernstein tell us that "Even a science lab is an aesthetic center. Using terms such as 'empathizing' or 'imaging' in all classes would automatically build transdisciplinary bridges" which could be "used to understand everything" (2000, p. A64).

In addition to expanding and honoring an aesthetic bank of ideas, teachers need to explore the sources of knowledge and raise questions about whose ideas infuse the work of art, the science experiment, the textbook, the cultural messages. In case after case, James W. Loewen, author of *Lies My Teacher Told Me*, compels us to consider how differently we would view slavery or the treatment of Native Americans if we understood that "history is a furious debate informed by evidence and reason," not a set of facts to be learned. The so-called objectivity of textbooks is a myth. History is as much about who is telling the story as the story itself. We have to question what is included and what is left out. Scientific exploration is not excluded. Teachers need to be scholars who recognize the hidden epistemology in all disciplines.

I recently asked a group of graduate students in education to write about a time when they were completely objective. After ten minutes, no one had written anything. Gone are the days when we asked teachers to leave their emotions and personal lives outside the classroom door for fear that the feeling part of a teacher's life would interfere with the essentials of learning. For generations, girls "learned" they couldn't do math as well as boys; children of color "learned" that they were inferior and disabled students "learned" that they were outsiders. As a result, many in each group behaved down to expectations. They not only failed the spelling test, but they thought of themselves as failures. Countee Cullen in his poem, "Incident," recalls how

> Once riding in old Baltimore. . .a boy stuck out his tongue and called me "Nigger...." I saw the whole of Baltimore, From May until December, Of all the things that happened there, That's all that I remember.

Teachers have to ask, "What lingers?"

I have read hundreds of essays written by college students describing the most important things they learned in school. Rarely are their narratives about the content of instruction. They learned about isolation, rejection, connection to someone who cared and personal recognition. Though schools are not necessarily the place where we actively go about teaching feelings, they are the settings where experiences are osmosed through membranes controlled by feelings.

Teaching and learning are all about this seamless emotional and intellectual self, the scientific and artistic components of our personal landscapes. To quote Maxine Greene, "It is important to hold in mind, therefore, that each of us achieved contact with the world from a particular vantage point, in terms of a particular biography" (1978, p. 2). Extending the argument, Paul Ehrlich, a professor of biological sciences, speaks of our cultural biography: "Our behaviors," he notes, "[r]esult from the interaction of our genetics and the cultures we inhabit. There is not a single human nature, any more than there is a single human genome, although there are features common to all human natures and all human genomes" (2000, p. 2). Countee Cullen says it another way, "Some teethe on a silver spoon, With the stars strung from a rattle; I cut my teeth as a black raccoon—For implements of battle." Each discipline brings a significant and necessary way of viewing the world. That is why teachers, artists and scientists need to acknowledge their own biographies, recognizing that as we go about doing our work in the world, our objectivity is compromised. So what? That is the reality.

Art Experiences: Catalysts for the Making of Meaning

Linda, a teacher in Columbia, South Carolina, does a performance piece about her experiences as an abused child using poetry, video, drama and music. The class is deeply moved by her aesthetically elegant and passionate presentation. Other students begin to speak about searing, personal experiences that have helped them come to know. I don't think that my classroom is becoming a confessional. I am convinced that the introduction of personal material clarifies the content and objectives of the course. An assumption about teaching and learning undergirds these projects. It is the belief that learners, most importantly teachers, need to explore how and why they came to know. It is downright dangerous to view teaching tethered only to the delivery of someone else's knowledge. Teaching and research rooted in students' ontological questions provide a bridge to the outside world. The stories we share may have common threads, but it is apparent that human nature varies in different geographies, time frames and cultures; there are human *natures.*

For Craig who has been teaching ten years in Pueblo, Colorado, the arts provided a safety net. He shares with the class excerpts from his elegantly written autobiography illustrated with photographs. The text is a personal document which emphasizes his working-class background. As James Olney (1972) tells us, when we walk back through our life, we transform how that life is perceived. Through print, body language and visuals, Craig imposes a new form on his personal world constructing and re-constructing how he came to know. Some students in the group discuss for the first time their own concerns about social class. The conversation is passionate, for Craig's depiction of his life not only dignifies and validates the "feeling facts" of his life but simultaneously authorizes others to reflect on the circumstances of their own cognition.

With a group of teachers, I visit a beautiful outdoor World War II Memorial in Olympia, Washington. Simon Kogen, the sculptor who designed the memorial, accompanies us. He explains that the 4000 cast bronze blades are wheat stalks, Washington's contribution to the war effort, and that they symbolize the men and women who died in the war. When you touch one blade, a chain reaction results, and a kind of musical soundscape is heard for five minutes. There is intense conversation about the ideas conveyed through this symbolic representation. A number of students share stories of relatives and friends who died during the war. In the emotional atmosphere that art experiences may evoke, teachers need to keep a watchful eye out that personal needs do not overwhelm the content of the course. In this situation, I did focus on the pedagogical implications of the shared experience. How were the teachers internalizing the experience? For some, it was the visual that dominated their thinking: the engraved

> names, the personal messages on the granite tiles, the beauty of the park. Others spoke about the sound as a pathway to memory and verbal expression. Teachers who had attended the deeply emotional dedication ceremony recalled the stories told at that time. The work of Howard Gardner in multiple intelligences was validated. It was through reliance on their strongest intelligence that each person made sense of the experience. Knowing that we can pull out our strong suit to meet new and often confusing situations, builds confidence and makes the strange, familiar.

Joe Kincheloe's emphasis on the integrative, purposive and negotiable aspects of the art experience helps me to see how these teachers captured meaning. When they transformed different domains of their experiences, they were reintegrating, in the Deweyian sense, their personal and professional lives. The personal experience was rich on another level, for in transforming the personal experience into public expression, it might be assimilated by others. James Olney's insights further reinforce how autobiographical writing functions as well as discriminates between the single metaphor that records a life as if its meaning were complete or the double metaphor that acknowledges that the act of writing one's life transforms the meaning of that life for the person who lives and writes it. This critical, non-reductionist approach to the arts is essential as a preparation for understanding the interrelationship of different curriculum areas, cultures and pedagogical processes.

Art Experiences: A Wedge for Recognizing the Similarities in the Human Condition

The following three extracts highlight encounters in theater and the visual arts which serve to link what we might view as ordinary (our own feelings) to a very different experience. Only the setting is extraordinary; the human response is completely identifiable.

> Two brothers, in Netanya, Israel, Avram and Joseph, one eighteen, the other twenty-four, present an improvised play about their family for a group of teachers taking a course on the Arts and Conflict Resolution. The boys' mother and father who are in the audience occasionally participate. The younger brother is retarded. Both brothers express feelings of outsiderness and rivalry. There is much yelling and pushing but also embracing. Their spoken and body languages reflect alternating anger, joy, togetherness and separateness. The boys break down the fourth wall of the theatre by throwing frequent questions to the audi-

ence. After the performance, many teachers express their surprise that a retarded boy is such a willing and competent actor and that his brother and parents are willing to engage in this very public performance. Aesthetic experiences illuminate socially shared concerns and may alter the personal attitudes of viewers and performers.

A class in "Education and Literacy" at Brooklyn College in New York City visits a museum and carefully examines illustrations done by Norman Rockwell. They depict an all-white America in the 1930s and 1940s. In another exhibit, they view the paintings of Jackson Pollack and other post-World War II abstract expressionists that display seemingly spontaneous drips, splashes and unique placements of color. The African American students in the group are not positively disposed to the Rockwell paintings, feeling that they are excluded from that all-white world. Others don't like the work of the expressionists because they, too, feel like outsiders. Not knowing what's going on, they reject the work. The sense is that both Norman Rockwell and the abstract expressionists belong to private clubs to which only a select few are given the password.

I am at the Studio Museum in Harlem with a group of teachers who view Whitfield Lovell's mixed media installation, "Whispers from the Walls." Inspired by the forced removal of a thriving African American community in 1921 because of fears about its proximity to a women's college in Denton, Texas, Lovell has constructed an intimate environment of layered voices, artifacts, portraits and musical sounds. We are there. We see a bed with a handmade quilt, a half-empty liquor decanter, a dead bird in a basket, family photographs. An old victrola is playing country blues. What pervades the scene is the memory of lives that have been disrupted, excluded and evicted from their homes. The sense of outsiderness pervades the ensuing and passionate discussion as people talk about their hunger to be on the inside. It is comforting to find "unmet" friends in literature and works of art. The challenge is to analyze personal experiences with concrete specificity while not losing the conceptual frames in which they can be grounded. The arts intensify the civic discourse as we acknowledge our empathy and personal connection to another's reality.

It is ironic that both the arts and education, philosophically committed to feeding the soul and intellect too often provide a carefully controlled regimen that lacks basic nutrients. For when the canonical requirements of the arts and educational establishments limit what is offered, many find themselves as starved outsiders. What should essentially be a community becomes a ghetto. Joe Kincheloe refers to this practice as "aesthetic policing." In education, these practices set up a hierarchy of curriculum cops who determine what is "necessary" information. The preceding narratives describe these feelings of marginality, alienation and speechlessness. It is as if the participants were invisible and their presence was nullified. If teaching is all about reflection, then doctrinaire canons are not good pedagogy. Education and the arts are condemned to freedom, which means not telling people what to think but empowering them with the tools to question.

References

Beckley, B. (Ed.). (1998). *Uncontrollable beauty: Toward a new aesthetics.* New York: Allworth Press.

Bly, R. (2001, January 1).The fish in the window. *The Nation*, p. 36.

Clark, K. B. (1965). *Dark ghetto: Dilemmas of power.* New York: Harper & Row.

Cullen, C. (1947). *On these I stand: An anthology of the best poems of Countee Cullen.* New York: Harper & Row.

Dewey, J. (1897). My pedagogic creed. In M. Dworkin (Ed.), *Dewey on education.* New York: Teachers College Press, 1959.

Ehrlich, P. (2000, September 9). Human natures: Genes, cultures and the human prospect. *The Chronicle of Higher Education*, p. 2.

Glover, J. (2001). *Humanity: A moral history of the twentieth century* New Haven: Yale University Press.

Greene, M. (1978). *Landscapes of learning.* New York: Teachers College Press.

Hoffman, D. (1998). *Visual intelligence: How we create what we see.* New York: Norton.

Johnson, E. S. (1965). Ways of knowing. In G. Hass & K. Wiles (Eds.) *Readings in curriculum.* Boston: Allyn & Bacon.

Kotlowitz, A. (1991). *There are no children here.* New York: Doubleday.

Kozol, J. (2000). *Ordinary resurrections: Children in the years of hope.* New York: Crown.

Loewen, James W. (1995). *Lies my teacher told me.* New York: New Press.

Noddings, N. (1992). *The challenge to care in schools: An alternative approach to education.* New York: Teachers College Press.

Olney, J. (1972). *Metaphors of self: The meaning of autobiography.* Princeton: Princeton University Press.

Root-Bernstein, R. S. & Root-Bernstein, M. (2000, January 14). Learning to think with emotion. *The Chronicle of Higher Education*, p. A64.

Rose, K. (1971). *A gift of the spirit.* New York: Holt, Rinehart and Winston.

Rose, M. (1990). *Lives on the boundary.* New York: Penguin Press.

Wright, Richard (1966). *Native son.* New York: Harper & Row, p. 10.

SIX

Not a Socratic Dialogue: No Final Solutions

Karel Rose and Joe L. Kincheloe

Throughout this book, Joe and I have sought to generate thought about the tensions and relationships that connect art, culture, politics, cognition and education. We have wondered and wandered in our attempts to embed artful pedagogy within these contexts while recognizing that the making of meaning is always a matter of contention. We are concerned that the values of the marketplace too frequently mediate what is taught in the schools under the banner of school-business partnerships. Corporate agendas subtly receive the imprimatur of the educational establishment, and the making of meaning is wrested from the teachers, learners and the community. At a time when educational quality is overrun with demands for more standardized testing, educators need to raise their voices in the discourse and expose how sound educational practices are eroded when they are caught in the net of observable facts, formulas and statistics (read test scores). Currently, more energy and anxiety are expended on the tests than on thinking about what knowledge is of most significance. We wonder whether the terrorist events of 2001 will not alter these priorities. Information should not be mistaken for knowledge, rhetoric for understanding and victory for truth. However, we do not wish to distance ourselves from practice for one test of theory is its connection to how we make meaning in the time and place of the worlds we inhabit.

The confusion is compounded in an information age where e-mail and chat rooms are both means and ends. Few people believe that they can move the mountain by carrying away very small stones. The behemoth of cyberspace makes them doubt their unspoken thoughts. The problem is compounded, as Joseph Urgo (2000) notes, when the importance of an interior life is denied by technologies (2000). Unquestionably, if time on task is the predominant value and multitasking often yields information rather than meaning, then reductionism and a monological delivery of unquestioned truths are most efficient. Our position is that if the source of meaning making is obfuscated as much by time constraints as by intention, a continuing dialogue is ultimately economical for the development of meaning.

We have reached a point where technology provides the language and metaphors for measuring the educational product. Standardization, test scores, earning potential and ultimate marketability are the templates for measuring success. It is no surprise that many students find it difficult to be reflective, analytical and creative. College graduates and undergraduates tell us that they dislike reading because it takes too much time. We are deeply concerned that the cultivation of higher order thinking skills will be abandoned for the measurable quick fix. It is far simpler to develop a test than to decide what and why we need to test. The tests begin to define the standards and the values rather than the reverse.

Multivoiced dialogues produce what Maxine Greene calls communal self-awareness. Experiences with the arts blur the boundaries that separate us from those whose cultures and worldviews may differ from our own. This is the democratizing power of aesthetic experience. Our students need not view the arts as remote encounters but as appropriate, integral aspects of their lives. Museums should not be forbidding temples where we passively gaze in awe and ponder the enormous prices and the number of security guards necessary for the safety of the treasures, but active places where engaged participants construct meaning. Museums, like schools, need to offer an equality of educational opportunities for all people, but visitor statistics and research studies show that museums are not experienced equally by all (Hooper-Greenhill, p. 22). We need to talk to teachers about how experiences with music, dance, theater and the visual arts help them to confront theeir personal and professional selves. Teachers need encouragement to crack the codes of what may feel like remote art and connect it to their lives. How does the dancing of the Urban Bushwomen help us to understand the patterns of street life and the pulsations of the city? How do Maori paintings illuminate the relationship between nature and emotion? How can a Hopper painting or a Plath poem give new meaning to the concept of loneliness?

Ongoing dialogue authorizes educators, children, families and communities to better understand their own voices and recognize how special interests and philosophical belief systems control what happens in schools. We have repeatedly explored some nagging questions throughout this book: What happens when teachers are silenced and denied a role in determining the curriculum and assessment procedures? Whose interests are best served by standardized tests? What do these tests test? Who determines what knowledge is most important? And finally how might encounters with the arts empower people to engage more authentically and knowledgeably in the world? A suitcase still stands in the hall waiting to be unpacked.

Joe and I are not seeking one answer but rather a range of possible responses. Those who argue well are not necessarily correct. A Socratic dialogue may provide grand rhetoric but be just sophistry. We respectfully decline to submit to anyone's last words, including our own. But this perspective does not take us off the hook. Educators need to search for truth and develop the language to argue persuasively—to express why the reduction of knowledge to test scores and observable proof is both educationally inefficient and inconsistent with democratic principles. In this context, we turn to aesthetic experiences with their potential for imaginative expression and intellectual growth.

Fortunately, we are not two lone wolves crying in the wilderness. Many segments of American culture do resist reductionist, boundaried thinking. It is unsettling to be in open opposition to mainstream culture but the gadfly role is an existential necessity to counter mindless homogeneity and powerlessness. Though teachers are not traditionally thought of as pot-stirrers, and some are reluctant and possibly embarrassed about advocating publicly for social change, it does not mean that they are not deeply offended by oppressive tactics. Many educators stand ready to re-think ideologies that are built on a false foundation of certainty and do stir the pot individually and collectively in their own classrooms and communities. They assign controversial books, introduce non-traditional and nonwestern perspectives, encourage students to support political movements and present art forms that challenge the acceptance of the marketplace logic.

In this book, we have turned to the arts to demonstrate how expressiveness enhances cognition and knowledge production. Feeling facts change lives. Learning is both a sensual and intellectual process that happens when we engage in play, tell stories, lay on hands, speak in new tongues, sing songs and respond with our bodies. The arts provide an entry point and connect to cognition by confronting the learner at all levels: sensory, intellectual, perceptual and political. Whimsy may provide the wedge. The work of a pop artist like Claes Oldenburg forces us to construct new meanings for familiar objects by altering their size, placement or texture. Giant pool balls are placed on the wall rather than the table; a Good Humor Bar is enlarged to monumental size, and a typewriter, constructed from soft materials, seems to have a persona. Making familiar objects strange is artful work, and the viewer along with the artist is pushed to transform her thinking. To know is to transform; to teach is to transform. Over time, everything is transformed: words, objects, facts, meanings, earth, space and civilization itself. How else could we have gotten from the fire to the toaster? Cave paintings to television sets? Rafts to ocean liners? Loincloths to suits? Scrolls to spreadsheets? Slavery to freedom? Aesthetic/cognitive questions are as much about human relationships in the world as they are about the objects that people create.

Transformative thinking, what Aristotle calls, "similarities in dissimilarities" is facilitated by aesthetic experience which links the rational and intuitive. According to a 1995 College Board profile of SAT and Achievement Takers, achievement test scores in academic subjects improved when the arts were used to assist learning in mathematics, creative writing and communication skills.

But even in this last chapter, the questions continue. We do not want the conversation to end for us or for our readers. Like Henry James, even after publication, we continue to edit. Grand conversations, verbally or in print, are the building blocks for grand actions. So, for now, some final questions.

Joe prefaces his first question with this statement: "We live in a country where the Puritan worldview is alive and well. The arts, still linked to wealth and leisure, are often defined as elitist, frivolous, non-intellectual and in some cases indecent. America continues to distrust the arts, most particularly non-Western and contemporary expressions, as a source of knowledge." Joe, you ask, "How can you answer the critics who say that if we haul the arts from the margins of educational practice to center stage, we will be retreating from intelligence and scholarly imagination?"

I think that it all revolves around your definition of scholar. I would define a scholar as someone who has a thinking disposition and a thirst to know the world, someone who has reflected on how personal and cultural forces have shaped her voice. A scholar, I believe, is someone who views scholarship and imagination as flip sides of the same coin, recognizing how the construction of new meanings blends the intellectual and sensual aspects of our being. A scholar breathes better when she is engaging with ideas. Ideas that are invigorated when she taps into her dreamy, mythical, spiritual and practical self. What Wordsworth calls the "inner eye" is fueled by an imaginative intellect. Diane Ackerman in *The Natural History of the Senses* (1990) eloquently describes the many ways our senses inspire our intelligence to consider new possibilities. Music spurs us to action; our own physical pain helps us to understand another's reality and synesthesia, that blending of the senses, invigorates our thoughts as well as our emotions. For teachers, this correspondence of the senses provides a delightful segue for examining the seamlessness of symbol systems. We can ask our students to write a poem about a painting, dance their names and associate colors with music. Students report that they can write for hours about a particular smell that releases a flood of memories. *Hailstone and Halibut Bones*, Mary O'Neill's delightful classic for children asks, "What is the color of love? of grandmothers? of summer?" Diane Ackerman quotes the synesthesia-loving writer Vladimir Nabokov, who is not "protected by more solid walls" and so analyzes what he calls his "colored hearing" (Ackerman, 1990). Many artists and teachers are keenly aware how the senses stimulate learning, retention, practical understandings and intelligence.

Intelligence, however, is a deeply problematic word. Joe, you have eloquently critiqued traditional assumptions of intelligence in *Rethinking Intelligence*. I am comfortable with your commitment to intelligence as a contextualized, cultural construction that has been shaped by powerful forces that are almost invisible. The implications for pedagogy and democracy are critical.

Here is another example of a teaching situation in which the arts provide a pedagogical opportunity to develop scholarly imagination and a heightened linguistic intelligence. In my undergraduate course in "Literacy and Education," students preparing to be teachers are each given a postcard of Andrew Wyeth's painting, "Christina's World." Initially they describe a rather grim rural scene with a disabled woman in the foreground dwarfed by a large yellowing field. She seems figuratively and literally imprisoned in this space by her infirmity. Students are asked to carefully cut out Christina and paste her into a very different world. The new world is a picture they've chosen from a magazine. The class ultimately creates a montage of environments that gives visual language their own cultural and psychological commitments. "I read incredible loneliness into the original picture," explains Lisa. "I placed Christina in a party environment. Though she is still very small, she is surrounded by smiling people." Melody's scene was not as comforting. Her picture was of a storm at sea, and Christina was on deck, crawling to safety. "I think that she's going to save herself," said Melody, "I know that I'm reflecting my own fears as well as my success in overcoming my personal demons." Each of the twenty-five new pictures presented a transformed world for Christina: antic, funny, fearsome, exotic and sexy. Everyone had made artistic decisions and recontextualized the subject. After all students had titled the picture and told their narratives, we created a sequential story using several pictures. Themes of journeys, struggle and freedom emerged. The landscapes were global and the stories reflected personal backgrounds. Some were recreating their own experiences; others imagined new stories. The process and the product honored free thinking.

Literary questions emerged from the aesthetic experience as students conflated their visual and verbal worlds. The act of telling was linked to the formation of memory, selecting and shaping the content. Questions surrounding character and context were paramount. How does setting alter meaning? The languages of visual art and literature merged. Figure, ground, character, mood, context and focus were words used interchangeably as an aesthetic experience translated into an exploration of self and how one accesses meaning.

Joe, your question was about intelligence and scholarly imagination. You reflect a pervasive concern in education today that students are not developing the necessary literacy skills to critically analyze and evaluate experience. In the "Christina activity," as the students considered the intentionality of the artist, they were simultaneously problematizing their own situation. Close examination of the picture enabled them to read the symbols: the clothes on a line, the yellowing field, Christina's gray hair and the position of her body. The exciting part was their own authorization, their respect for imaginative ways of knowing. The artist's intention may shape the viewer's response but does not limit it. For when Christina is placed in a new world, she is transformed into the subject of a new creator.

As students orally and in writing express ideas, they are leaping from imagination into linguistic expression. This encoding process suggests a map for the way we think. Though teachers need workable schemata for instruction, learning, itself, is a collage. Integrating literacy learnings with the senses is a powerful tool for developing thoughtful, engaged readers at any level. Robert and Michele Root-Bernstein (2000) note that Albert Einstein stated, "that after he had (first) solved his problems visually and kinesthetically, conventional words or other signs (were the) second stage." This search for equivalents in different modalities is a highly intellectual process and suggests pedagogical possibilities.

Other literacy understandings emerged from the "Christina work." The significance of context grounded the activity but also segued into a discussion of cultural influences and the meaning of time and place. We were also reinforcing the skills essential for oral and written literacy: attention to detail, noting sequence, making inferences. In creating their stories, students were organizing experiences narratively, responding to beginnings, endings, tensions, cycles and themes as well as recognizing multiple ways of representing experiences. The process of visually altering Christina's world necessitates thought about symbol systems that do not rely solely on oral and written responses. Indeed, the difficulty that so many children have with reading is understanding that words are merely symbols for things, abstractions, not the thing itself.

Pedagogically, this was a collaborative activity. The students, individually and in groups participated with each other taking control of the learning process. When they read the visual images, they were decoders; when they transformed images into their stories, they were encoders. They played the multiple roles of artist, viewer, teacher and learner. An aesthetic experience provided the pathway for getting in touch with partially understood ideas.

Aesthetic Experience and Thinking

Joe asks: Karel, throughout this book, we have drawn many parallels between the work of artists and teachers. I think that we have agreed that both the artist and the teacher do their work because they are impelled to do so but also so that they can convince, inspire and in some cases persuade others to some kind of action. But are there similarities in the ways the artist and the teacher go about their work? My questions revolve around the notion of teacher as artist. Does a teacher think about pedagogy as an artist thinks about his or her work? What are the implications for cognition when education is aestheticized?

I have always wondered what it takes to grow an artist. Why are some people mesmerized by the arts and others seduced by the sciences? Chapter 5 looked at some of the ways the arts and sciences are coupled. How does a Mary Cassatt, George Gershwin, Barbara Beach or Renee Queen choose a life's work? In case you don't recognize the last two names, they are superb, artful teachers. It would seem that many teachers and artists do not segregate their life and their work. They suck up experiences like a giant vacuum cleaner and convert them into new forms. When imagination and intellect meet, it may blossom in a poem, a ballet or a lesson plan. Artful, creative people are sensualists alert to everything around them. They are voyeurs and very little escapes their attention. They are eavesdroppers, visual detectives, memoirists, collectors of things, words and sensations. Ben Shahn, an important American artist, had this advice for his colleagues: "Never be afraid to become embroiled in art or life or politics" (Herberholz 1964, p. 9). The work of teachers, writers, composers, athletes, CEO's, parents all demand thoughtfulness as well as the ability to improvise and trust the process. Donald Schön

(1987) in his work on reflective practitioners encourages teachers to rid themselves of blueprints. He is not suggesting that they abandon any plan of action but rather that they recognize more fully the audience, the artist's place in the process and the contextual demands of the subject.

Teachers and artists are concept makers who bring new forms into being. This is where the implications of aesthetic experiences for cognition become apparent. Let us compare the work of a dancer and a teacher. Though the dancer and teacher communicate in different languages, they both honor expressiveness as a path to learning. The work of Howard Gardner, Erik Erikson and Robert Kegan tells us that what is experienced physically and concretely may be later understood abstractly. Maria Montessori, the early childhood educator, understood the physical and sensual connections to cognition when she had preschoolers, among other activities, trace sandpaper letters with their fingers. Meaning making in all modalities requires understanding of nonprint languages and abstract concepts. Experiences with movement, the creation of gesture, encounters with the symbolic language of dance (grasping, pointing, and so forth) provide entry points for understanding print. Letters, words and movements mean something. Children at a very young age "read" symbolic language: the McDonald's sign, the logo on their friend's sneakers, a raised fist, a mother's grimace.

Let's look at a group of preservice teachers at Lincoln Center Institute in New York City learning about dance. The work under study is *Flamenco Vivo*. Diane Ramo is the teaching artist, but she does not begin with the dance itself. She enters movement through language. Some teachers may do it differently, using non-verbal modes of expression as a segue into language. A teaching artist's conversation might go something like this: "How many of you enjoy watching dance? How many of you like to dance? Have any of you danced Flamenco?" Students are invited to recall other times when their bodies felt free. Connecting to previous experience in a different context, they arrange that new information into a preexisting slot. Prior knowledge is activated. As students speak about their previous experiences with dance, they free the relevant ideas or schemata. You wouldn't have students read *The Scarlet Letter* before building on prior knowledge about community attitudes, the meaning of adultery, women's roles and the historical context. Though gesture and movement may often replace words, it is the recollection of previous embodied experiences that facilitates the construction of meaning. Frequently, sensory images provide the pathway back to earlier understandings. Though none of us may be Marcel Proust, who smelled the madeleines in a Paris bakery and recalled a lifetime of experiences in a masterpiece, sensuous experiences, throughout our lives can heighten our aesthetic and cognitive abilities by catalyzing visual and verbal memory.

There are many similarities between the work of the artist and the teacher. The teacher of reading for example does not begin with the text itself. It is necessary first to activate prior knowledge, recalling through thought and image, previous experiences. Both the artist and the teacher build on schema theory and open what Lev Vygotsky terms *the zone of proximal development*, helping students to place the new information in a preexisting slot. When students speak about previous experiences with dance and remember the clicking heels, the rhythmic music, they are freeing the relevant ideas (schemata). They will do the very same kind of work as teachers when they introduce Harry Potter and ask children what they know about sorcerers. As we deconstruct the pedagogy of a teaching artist, its relevance for teachers becomes apparent. Activating prior knowledge enhances meaning making, and though the schemata may differ, both require the learner to tap into their own backgrounds.

A dancer speaks of the palette of possibilities in her own lexicon: gesture, posture, movement, rhythm, tableaux. A teacher concerned about spoken and written understandings develops thought using symbol systems that focus on words and phrases that describe literary constructs such as plot, mood and character. But both the artist and the teacher work with abstract concepts designed to develop cognitive competence.

The work of teachers and artists is complex because it requires the transformation of experience into other symbol systems. Teachers translate social issues, texts, historical events, personal experiences and current events in a classroom space. Artists may do their translations in a studio, outdoors, or in a corner of a loft. Both use a variety of materials, media and modes of expression. Gestural language provides a powerful assist. In much the way that a choreographer transposes ideas with planned movements, teachers must transform experience into understandable and rich symbol systems. The active reading of dance movement shares similarities with the active reading of literature. Encoding and decoding are essential cognitive activities for the artist and the teacher.

Joe, we ask together whether the appalling events of 2001 will alter the way in which we respond to our world. At a time when we need the highest level of intelligence and scholarly imagination, has American education prepared our leaders and citizenry? Our history is replete with myths. Our dailiness had not previously included a physically fractured city except on the television screen. Where do we go from here? There are no comfortable answers, but we do know that our children must be provided with the most complete, integrated and global education, intellectually and aesthetically.

Joe, here's a question for you. You seem to be fascinated with the relationship between art and cognition. How does artful teaching move us to new levels of cognition? What might that mean?

Yes, I am obsessed with this relationship, believing that at various points along the borders where art, artful teaching and cognition intersect there rest some great possibilities for advancements in human thinking. What we have been writing about in this book under the titles of art and artful teaching can be characterized by Maxine Greene's (1988) concept of a "new commitment to intelligence" and its cultivation. Art that is contextually considered makes such a commitment possible, it opens up the topic to imaginative conversation. As you maintained earlier in this dialogue, higher-order thinking is under attack from reductionistic educational reformers and their ideological frameworks.

As we operate in the post-September 11 world, I closely watch the U.S. news media produce information about the tragedy and the events surrounding it. Rarely in this context do we hear a diversity of opinions, challenges to see the world from different vantage points or calls to analyze the history of American relationships with the Muslim world over the last few centuries. Put in the lexicon of this book, higher order thinking about the meaning of these events is simply not a part of this life-and-death public conversation. In this informational reality, Karel, your concept of the instrumental value of art with its ability to make us better students, teachers and scholars becomes even more important. Becoming a better scholar and attaining a higher order of cognition are inseparable concepts. It is impossible to determine where one ends and the other begins.

Too much art pedagogy and education in general involve producing students who know only what power wielders and teachers want them to know. The positivistic and psychometric forms of teaching that dominate the twenty-first century educational landscape are of this variety, as they discount the cultivation of higher orders of thinking. Artful teaching induces us to move beyond these limiting ways of thinking about thinking. Even in art education itself, this reductionistic form of cognition seems to dominate the process. In this context, the artist stands in isolation from other disciplines of knowledge and the larger society. This marginalized figure is romanticized and viewed as a cultural icon separate from the lived reality of everyday life. The instrumental value of art and its contributions to higher orders of cognition are intentionally discarded. Comparisons and relationships between the types of cognition encouraged by diverse disciplines and aesthetic modes of thinking are also irrelevant in this context.

In the reductionism of positivist teaching there exists an assumption that what is most important is an unchanging, essential body of knowledge to be transferred in correct sequence to the student. Such a way of conceptualizing teaching does not allow for multiple perspectives, viewpoints from, for example, Africa, from Native Americans or from indigenous artists from around the world. Here we go back to the notions of cognitive cubism developed earlier, where like Duchamp we gain the cognitive benefits from viewing a phenomenon from a number of perspectives. As we catch the bus of multiple perspectives on our journey to a higher order of cognition, we historicize our insights with understandings of multiple traditions, the sociocultural divisions that shape them and the power relations that inscribe them. Here rests a sleeping higher order of cognition, forced into hibernation by right-wing impulses and positivist ways of reasoning and teaching. Our job, of course, is to awaken this cognitive *ursus horribilis*.

Until the big bear is roused many will be incapable of posing questions, teaching lessons and thinking outside of a cardboard container constructed by truncated academic disciplines with monologics that reflect the cognitive frames of one group of people operating at a specific historical juncture. In this cognitive context, conventional meanings are rarely challenged, the wishes of power remain in tact and the relationship between art and cognition is static. In light of the concerns you have expressed with art and standardization in this educational *Zeitgeist*, Karel, art in this truncated cognitive context becomes a codified body of indestructible knowledge. Such normalized knowledge was here yesterday, is here today, and will be here tomorrow no matter what the hell happens. This knowledge of art and ways of teaching and thinking implicit within it were produced at those official places where meaning is made and perpetuated. Lanny Beyer (2000) challenges this power-saturated making of meaning by arguing that the arts produce possibilities for considering and thinking about the viewpoints and values of other people. Thus, art, artful teaching and the cognition that accompanies them can provide evocative confrontations with difference.

The obvious example that I used earlier in the book involves non-Western postcolonial liberation movements and the self-representations of African, Asian, Latin American and various indigenous peoples from around the world. Such representations provided a sometimes shocking confrontation with difference that held profound cognitive consequences—life-changing consequences—for many Westerners. Indeed, these self-representations of non-Western people can be considered one of the most important cognitive experiences of the last century. Still, of course, the lesson didn't "take" with many Westerners. Instead of learning from it, they ran away and sought shelter in a return to a monolithic Western canon and the ethnocentrism it promoted. These frightened scholars and politicos were far more comfortable operating within the boundaries of a truncated cognition and the demeaning versions of "others" that it embraces. Ah, the comfort of home, of artistic and cognitive agoraphobia. Lord, they pray, keep us away from those "shock artists" and their rude demands to reflect on our assumptions about the art, the world and its people. Cognitive overload—delete—give me the cognitive comfort of the traditional canon, they insist. Unfortunately, after the experiences of September 2001 a few individuals in the West gained a new insight into the need for such reflection about our cultural, political, cognitive, economic, historical and aesthetic assumptions. A few individuals gained new perspectives on how such assumptions are perceived in the Muslim world in particular.

Joe, given your response above, what does it mean to employ higher order thinking in relation to our concept of artful teaching?

I've been working on the answer to this question for the last 25 years. In my work on postformal thinking, I've attempted to develop a vision of what it means to operate at a higher cognitive order. Upon this foundation, I've argued, we can build both a complex form of pedagogy, a model for rigorous scholarship and a grounding for new approaches to research (see Ray Horn, 2000). One of the most basic concepts in this move to a higher order of cognition connects directly to the views of art and artful teaching that we have developed here. Being able to see and perceive in multiple ways is necessary for a great artist, an artful teacher and higher order thinkers in general. To see self, objects, students ad infinitum from multiple perspectives and in the process discern the significance of each perspective and, importantly, their relationship to one another rests at the heart of expanded forms of cognition.

In this expanded cognitive context, perceptions of new levels of complexity are possible. Awareness of new orders of complexity leads to a new understanding of contradictions and the way they shape artistic work and interpretation, the classroom and the world-at-large. The world of art often helps us understand this notion of contradiction. Indeed, the art world itself constantly reflects contradiction as we see creative and cognitively sophisticated artists interact with the specters of monoculturalism, ethnocentrism, patriarchy, class elitism and commodification to name only a few. The contradiction that emerges as art establishmentarians and educators refuse to contextualize the artistic and aesthetic processes historically, socially, culturally, politically, ideologically, discursively, economically, rhetorically or philosophically always eats away at the energy and vitality of artistic production and art pedagogy. The boundaries of higher order cognition are tightened by this lack of attention to the contradiction and the role of art in the larger culture is diminished.

Without awareness of the need for contextualization, there is no warrant for us to argue that students of art—like all students—need the benefits of rigorous research skills to explore the subject matters of their productions. Without these insights and abilities, artists, art educators and teachers of all stripes do not possess the cognitive sophistication to connect their art and their pedagogies to current political questions. In this truncated context, they are blind to the multiple confluences of artistic production and the market, the insidious ways tyrannical states have employed art for their own nefarious interests and in the twenty-first century the ways corporate power wielders use art to enhance their power. Higher orders of cognition in this context always search for connections between art and other disciplinary and transdisciplinary dynamics in the quest for unique insights.

This inability to see art in context—so characteristic of the "Sensation" exhibit controversy in 1999—reappeared in New York in early 2001, instigated once again by Mayor Rudolph Giuliani. Artist Renee Cox's "Yo Mama's Last Supper," included as one photograph in the Brooklyn Museum's exhibition of a collection of 188 photographs by African American photographers, is a nude picture of Cox as the Christ figure at the Last Supper surrounded by eleven black and one white apostle. Giuliani labeled the photograph "disgusting, outrageous, and anti-Catholic" and promised to explore the possibility of litigation against and criminal penalties for Cox and the Brooklyn Museum. This is when Giuliani proposed his "commission on decency" to set standards for public art (Bumiller, 2001).

Cox stated that the picture was a commentary on her experiences as a female, black Catholic and sought to shed light on the gender bias and racism of the Catholic Church. The mayor and many of his supporters seemed unable or unwilling to consider the contextualized role of art as a manifestation of the higher order of cognition presented here. The understanding of this important dimension of artistic relationships to the compelling social, political, cultural, economic, religious and philosophical questions of the day falls outside the cognitive-ideological frames of mainstream ways of viewing the aesthetic dimension. In this reductionistic context individuals are ideologically blinded to the ways they themselves and human beings in general are social productions of our individual experiences as they intersect with macro-social structures. Only with this understanding can individuals such as Giuliani begin the cognitively complex take of examining their ethnocentrism and locating themselves in the narratives of history.

Karel, I maintain that Giuliani provides us with a profound example of what happens when one is unable or unwilling to move to the higher order cognitive processes under discussion. In addition to the contextualizing and connecting abilities previously noted, Giuliani lacks a sense of historicity. By historicity I mean to denote the specific ability to relate the particularity of private experience to larger historical patterns and processes. In this higher order cognitive context, Giuliani could begin to reflect on his own Catholic Italian experiences. In this analytical context, he might begin to understand the difference, for example, between his own historically constructed views of Catholicism, the purposes of art and the world in general and those of Renee Cox as an African American woman. In the complexities and contradictions of these different experiences, Giuliani might begin to understand why Cox feels as she does, uses art as she does and why she might produce a piece such as "Yo Mama's Last Supper."

Armed with such appreciations, Giuliani might come to understand how "Yo Mama's Last Supper" can shed light on the origins, construction and social implications of his own viewpoints. Because of his emerging sense of historicity, his awareness of his own and other people's placement in history, Giuliani might be ready to reconsider his use of the terms *disgusting*, *outrageous* and *anti-Catholic* to describe Cox's photograph. This complex sense of historicity, so important in cognitive development involves the act of placing ourselves, our political perspectives, our religious beliefs, our art and our teaching in the web of reality. For example, when I read E. D. Hirsch's (1988) construction in his book, *Cultural Literacy*, of what essential knowledge American citizens should know, I was amazed at how his location as a white, upper middle-class, American male shaped his choice of knowledge. Most of the content was made up of data about white, upper/upper middle-class males from a Western heritage.

A more sophisticated mode of cognition informed by historicity might have helped Hirsch reflect on the ways his location in the web of reality, his personal experiences, his cultural knowledges, shaped his perspectives. Artful teaching is based on a cognition of complexity. A cognition of complexity teaches us about the social world's complicated web-like configuration of interacting forces. Artistic producers and knowledge producers, like all of us, are entangled in, not disengaged from the web. The principle of complexity asserts that knower and known are inseparable—both part of the web of reality. No teacher, no artist, no scholar in this web-like configuration of the cosmos can achieve a God-like perspective; no one can totally escape the web and look back on it from afar.

We must all confess our socially constructed nature and our resulting subjectivity. To become higher order thinkers we must recognize our limited vantage point—all of us, Joe Kincheloe, Karel Rose, E. D. Hirsch, Renee Cox and Sir Rudolph Giuliani. These are the lessons of historicity that are so important for artful teachers. Artful teachers know that reductionism and the artistic productions, aesthetic interpretations and the pedagogies it supports ignore the way our historicity shapes our consciousness. As a result our concept of the social, artistic and educational worlds is stripped of its complexity and reduced to a static, one-dimensional frame. Thus, released from the complications of historicity, reductionistic artistic producers, researchers and teachers feel confident that they can produce timeless art, make precise predictions, pass along the simple truth to their students and ignore the interactive process in which all social activity is grounded.

In this complex, higher order cognitive context, for example, art producers, scholars and teachers refuse to accept or reject the truth claims of any analysis without considering its discursive nature. This involves: where the analysis comes from in the web of reality; which analyses can be officially transmitted and which cannot; and who transmits the analyses and who listens. Without such reflections art producers, scholars and teachers travel through life imprisoned by the prejudices derived from everyday existence or by what is often labeled common sense. The habitual beliefs of an individual's historical age become tyrants to minds unable to reflect on their genesis. Students, for example, emerge from sixteen to twenty years of schooling without having been asked to think about our own thinking. In this situation individuals are unprepared to meet the demands of becoming groundbreaking artists, rigorous scholars, inspiring teachers, or engaged citizens.

Because a complex, higher order cognition moves individuals to new levels of understanding of the social structures, discursive strategies, ideologies and psychological dynamics that move human events and shape institutions, such people often see things that others don't see. As you maintained earlier in this dialogue, Karel, it is disturbing to stand in opposition to one's professional culture or to be out of step with mainstream thinking—but this is exactly what the artful teacher sometimes has to do. In this context, one must be psychologically healthy to deal with the stress of such a stance. At the very least, students, artists and prospective teachers must understand the psychic burden that artful teaching as we have described it here often demands. An artful teacher, for example, because of her understanding of the monological ethnocentrism of the art discourse presented in curriculum guides and textbooks, may find herself under suspicion from her peers and superiors because of her oppositional stance.

Here the act of rigorous thinking with its sociopolitical contextualization, search for the origins of ascribed meanings, analysis of patterns of exclusion and use of a variety of methodological modes of analysis operationalizes itself as oppositionality. I have tried often in the quest for smooth interpersonal relations to get around this reality; sometimes I can, sometimes I cannot. As our understanding of the past intersects with our vision of the future, whether we like it or not our relationship to the present is changed. As you so correctly assert and demonstrate in your teaching, Karel, in the artistic context this relationship to the present cannot be separated from structures of feelings and emotions. Artful teaching is not simply a rational process; contrary to popular perception higher order thinking is an emotional as well as a logical process.

Higher-order thinking, especially in its postformal articulation, demands that art, pedagogy, emotion, history and cognition be integrated for synergistic effects. At this point we return to our notion of a complex aesthetics and the types of thinking the artistic experience makes possible. Here we reaffirm the complex aesthetic principles of integration and connection, exposure of the process of social construction of artistic knowledge and the need to challenge accepted artistic categories as final truths. Without these features of complex artistic thinking, we fall into the same old trap over and over again. New art that is engaged with the lived politics of the world debuts, but the public conversation about it is unable to proceed because of the absence of these understandings.

How infrequently political or media figures ask an artist how his or her work addresses the political context or the vicissitudes of everyday life. The realms of popular media and their knowledge production and the world of art remain forever separate, disengaged, isolated spheres. In this context the American public loses, as it is "protected" from the challenges of a complex aesthetics, the higher order cognition it promotes and the sociopolitical and cultural engagement it demands. Living in fear, the art world and art education tiptoe around these potential challenges, hoping they will just go away. Questions of art in relation to feeling and moral values seem, amazingly, out of place in this context; a complex aesthetics appears to many as a concept from another dimension of space and time. Art controversy after art controversy comes and goes: In recent years Maplethorpe, Andres Serrano, Dread Scott, "Sensation," Renee Cox are merely a few. Yet the lessons of a higher order of cognition about art and the notion of a complex aesthetics are not publicly discussed. Do we now begin to understand the ways power operates?

References

Ackerman, D. (1990). *A natural history of the senses.* New York: Vintage Books.

Beyer, L. (2000). *The arts, popular culture, and social change.* New York: Peter Lang.

Bumiller, E. (2001). Affronted by nude "Last Supper," Giuliani calls for Decency Panel. *New York Times,* February 16 http://www.nytimes.com/2001/02/16/arts/16/muse.html

The college board profile of SAT and achievement test takers. (1995). *Eloquent evidence: Arts at the core of learning.* National Endowment for the Arts.

Greene, M. (1988). *The dialectic of freedom.* New York: Teachers College Press.

Herberholz, Donald W. & Herberholz, B. (1964). *Artworks for elementary teachers: Developing artistic and perceptual awareness.* Dubuque, IA: Wm. C. Brown.

Hirsch, E. D. (1988). *Cultural literacy.* New York: Vintage Books.

Hooper-Greenhill, E. (1999). *The educational role of the museum.* New York: Routledge.

Horn, R. (2000). *Teacher talk: A postformal inquiry into educational change.* New York: Peter Lang.

O'Neill, M. (1989). *Hailstones and halibut bones: Adventures in color.* New York: Philomel.

Root-Bernstein, R.S. & Root-Bernstein, M. (2000, 14), Learning to think with emotion. *The Chronicle of Higher Education,* p. A64.

Schön, D. (1987). *Educating the reflective practitioner.* San Francisco: Jossey-Bass.

Urgo, J. R. (2000). *In the age of distraction.* Jackson, Mississippi: University Press of Mississippi.

APPENDIX

CONTINUING THREATS AGAINST ART

DREAD SCOTT

Let's start with the obvious. It is outrageous and dangerous for the government to try and crush a major cultural institution and through this set a precedent for future action because the mayor doesn't like the content of one of the institution's exhibits. If they succeed this will send a long-lasting chill through the art world.

Ten years ago, George Bush denounced my art, and the U.S. Congress passed legislation that in part outlawed it because of my use of the American flag. The government was trying to prescribe one government-approved use and interpretation of the flag. With his threats against the Brooklyn Museum, Giuliani is trying to use the force of government to enforce traditional Christian values on society. Giuliani said, "If they think that it's necessary to throw feces on important national and religious symbols, then they should pay for it themselves?" The Virgin Mary isn't a national symbol, but for Giuliani she should be. Giuliani apparently wants a society where there is only one government-approved representation of the Virgin Mary, presumably a sixteenth-century Renaissance white virgin. Well, if Chris Ofili, an artist of Nigerian descent, wants a black Virgin, and he and other young artists want to question these traditional values, more power to them.

This whole controversy is taking place at a time when the Christian Right has outlawed the teaching of evolution in Kansas, and fundamentalist Christians are having shooting sprees at Jews and people of color in California and Illinois, murdering abortion providers and blowing up government office buildings. Put bluntly, beyond attempting to extend governmental control of the arts, Giuliani is pandering to this ugly reactionary element in society. This is a mayor whose police routinely brutalize and murder people, and he finds nothing wrong with this. Now Giuliani wants to police the art world. Many in the arts have taken the hint: "Be afraid, be very afraid." But what is needed now is courage.

Fortunately, in the face of severe governmental threats, the Brooklyn Museum has had the courage not to back down. Beyond this, other art institutions and artists have finally taken a good stand on this and have come to the defense of the BMA. Artists and people generally are counting on you not to back down even if the intimidation increases. One thing that I have learned from the various efforts to censor and suppress my art is that it is possible to defeat attempts at censorship, but you must show courage in the face of threats, and others will be strong if you remain strong. Together we can win.

But beyond winning this battle in the Culture Wars, what this whole controversy shows is that what is really needed is a climate of resistance, resistance to Giuliani's and others' reactionary attempt to enforce traditional values on us and to the larger political agenda which this latest effort is a part of. And I think artists have a special role we can play in helping forge this climate of resistance. I'm a member of Refuse and Resist's Artist Network. We are artists in many media and genres who are determined to build a culture of resistance. Instead of just calling for First Amendment Rights, let's oppose the reactionary lifeless world that Rudy and Company are trying to create with an atmosphere that cherishes, calibrates and defends a vibrant culture of resistance. Let's sing our own song. Imagine galleries and museums, concert halls and theaters across the country all filled with art that defies the censors and drives the Giulianis of the world back into their caves. Join us in this mission.

INDEX

www.ingramcontent.com/pod-product-compliance
Ingram Content Group UK Ltd.
Pitfield, Milton Keynes, MK11 3LW, UK
UKHW020159290926
15471UKWH00005B/964

9 780820 457451